Satellite Hacking: Cybersecurity Threats in Space IoT Systems

Zephyrion Stravos

Introduction: Welcome to the Final Frontier of Hacking!

You ever stare up at the night sky, see a tiny blinking dot cruising through the stars, and think, I wonder if I could hack that? No? Just me? Well, congratulations, you're about to develop a brand-new obsession.

Welcome to **Satellite Hacking: Cybersecurity Threats in Space IoT Systems**, the latest addition to the *IoT Red Teaming: Offensive and Defensive Strategies series*. If you've been with me through **Mastering Hardware Hacking, Firmware Hacking & Reverse Engineering**, or my personal favorite, **The Car Hacker's Guide** (where we may or may not have discussed how to make your neighbor's Tesla play nothing but whale sounds), then you already know what you're in for—high-energy, hands-on hacking with a splash of sarcasm and a metric ton of technical mischief.

But this time, we're leaving Earth behind.

So, You Want to Hack a Satellite?

First off, let's get one thing straight: hacking satellites isn't like popping open a Wi-Fi router or spoofing a smart thermostat. There's no "Ctrl+Alt+Hack" button to press. These things are floating hundreds—sometimes thousands—of kilometers above us, moving at 28,000 km/h, and designed to withstand radiation that would turn your laptop into a glowing paperweight.

Yet, despite all that high-tech wizardry, satellites have security flaws—some of them terrifyingly simple to exploit. And if there's one thing I've learned in this field, it's that if something can be hacked, someone will hack it. That someone might as well be you (for educational and legal purposes, of course… probably).

Attack of the Space Hackers

If you think satellite hacking is just science fiction, think again. In 2022, Elon Musk's Starlink got hit with a $25 homemade hacking rig. In 2007, Chinese hackers reportedly took control of US satellites. And if history has taught us anything, it's that once something is connected to the internet, it's only a matter of time before someone tries to break it.

Satellites are no different. From GPS spoofing that can reroute ships and planes to signal jamming that can disable military communications, the stakes are sky-high (pun absolutely intended). And as the Space IoT boom continues—bringing self-driving rovers, interplanetary Wi-Fi, and even cloud computing to the great beyond—more vulnerabilities are going to emerge.

That's where you come in.

What's in This Book?

This book isn't a dry, theoretical breakdown of satellite security. Oh no, we're getting our hands dirty. By the time you finish, you'll have a working knowledge of:

- How modern satellites work (without needing a PhD from NASA)
- How hackers find and track satellites using public data
- How to intercept, jam, and even spoof satellite signals
- How to attack and secure satellite ground stations
- How to protect space IoT systems from cyber threats

Whether you're a penetration tester, security researcher, or just a curious tech enthusiast who wants to know how the real-world Space Force battles hackers, this book is for you.

The Legality of Space Shenanigans

Now, before you get any wild ideas about hijacking a weather satellite just to make it rain on your ex's wedding, let's talk legal stuff.

Hacking satellites without permission is a one-way ticket to a windowless room in a federal facility. I don't care how cool you think you are with your SDR kit—goofing around with unauthorized signals can get you in some serious FCC, ITU, and Outer Space Treaty-level trouble. That's why this book is strictly educational. We're here to understand threats, not create intergalactic incidents.

Why This Book? Why Now?

Space used to be the playground of governments and billion-dollar corporations. Now? It's the Wild West.

With the rise of SpaceX, OneWeb, Amazon Kuiper, and a growing army of DIY satellite hackers, the attack surface is expanding faster than ever. This isn't some far-off, futuristic problem—satellite cybersecurity is an issue today. If you're in cybersecurity, this knowledge isn't just useful, it's critical.

Also, let's be honest... hacking space tech just sounds cool.

Strap In. It's Going to Be a Wild Ride.

If this is your first book in the IoT Red Teaming series, welcome to the rabbit hole. If you've already survived Wireless Hacking Unleashed or Hacking Medical IoT, you know the drill—grab your SDR, fire up your terminal, and prepare to exploit, defend, and demystify one of the most exciting frontiers in cybersecurity.

Let's get started. 🚀

Chapter 1: Introduction to Satellite Cybersecurity

You ever watch a sci-fi movie where a hacker takes control of a satellite with a few keystrokes and think, Pfft, Hollywood nonsense? Well, surprise—it's not that far from reality. Sure, you won't be rerouting satellites with a laptop from your mom's basement, but you can exploit vulnerabilities in outdated protocols, weak encryption, and exposed ground stations. The world of satellite cybersecurity is a mix of high-tech wizardry and shockingly bad security practices, and in this chapter, we're diving headfirst into it.

Satellite systems are critical to modern communication, navigation, and even national security, yet they remain one of the most overlooked areas in cybersecurity. This chapter introduces the fundamentals of satellite security, including the attack surfaces, major threats like jamming and spoofing, and the legal landscape governing space technology. We'll also explore how researchers set up labs to test these vulnerabilities—because understanding the threats is the first step in securing them.

1.1 Overview of Modern Satellite Systems and Space IoT

Welcome to the Age of Space Junk and Hackable Satellites

Let's be honest—when most people think of satellites, they picture giant, futuristic machines floating majestically in space, beaming down ultra-secure signals to make our lives better. But in reality? It's more like a scrapyard of aging tech, weak encryption, and vulnerabilities waiting to be exploited.

Right now, there are over 8,000 active satellites orbiting Earth, doing everything from powering your GPS to helping farmers decide when to water their crops. Then there's the mountain of dead satellites, space debris, and abandoned hardware drifting around, making low Earth orbit (LEO) look like a cosmic junkyard. And here's the kicker—many of the satellites still in use are running on decades-old technology. Imagine trying to secure a critical global communication system that's still running Windows XP or, worse, some proprietary firmware from the 1980s. That's the reality of modern satellite systems.

Now, enter the new era: Space IoT. Yep, just like your smart fridge can tell you when you're out of milk, satellites are now part of the ever-growing Internet of Things (IoT). But just like your smart fridge is hackable (yes, really), so are these satellites. More connectivity means more attack surfaces, and if there's one thing hackers love, it's poorly secured, highly valuable systems floating thousands of miles above Earth.

So, before we start breaking into satellite networks (ethically, of course), let's break down how these systems actually work and why they're so vulnerable to attack.

The Anatomy of a Modern Satellite System

To understand how to hack (or secure) satellites, you need to know what they're made of. A modern satellite system isn't just the spacecraft itself—it's an entire ecosystem made up of:

- **Satellites in Orbit** – These can be anything from a massive geostationary communication satellite the size of a bus to tiny CubeSats no bigger than a shoebox.
- **Ground Stations** – The command centers that send and receive signals, update software, and make sure the satellite isn't just floating around uselessly.
- **Relay Stations & Gateways** – Used to transfer data between satellites and ground systems, sometimes acting as an extra "hop" to cover larger distances.
- **User Devices** – Everything from military GPS units to your car's navigation system depends on satellite data.

These systems work together to provide internet, navigation, imaging, and military intelligence, but each part of the ecosystem also introduces new attack vectors. Hackers don't need to break into a satellite directly—they can target ground stations, hijack signal relays, or spoof data that end-user devices rely on.

The Rise of Space IoT: More Satellites, More Problems

The number of satellites in orbit is exploding thanks to SpaceX, Amazon's Project Kuiper, OneWeb, and other commercial players launching massive constellations of small satellites. These Low Earth Orbit (LEO) satellites are used for everything from global broadband internet to environmental monitoring and military surveillance.

And while this is great for faster internet and global connectivity, it also means:

- **More Targets** – More satellites = more opportunities for hackers.
- **More Wireless Communication** – LEO satellites rely on RF signals and laser communication, both of which can be intercepted, jammed, or spoofed.
- **More Software-Defined Satellites** – Unlike old-school hardware-locked satellites, many modern ones allow software updates, meaning attackers can try to inject malicious code remotely.

And let's not forget the biggest issue with IoT security: manufacturers prioritize speed and cost over security. When companies are racing to deploy thousands of satellites, they don't always invest in securing them properly.

Why Are Satellites So Vulnerable to Hacking?

You'd think that something as critical as a satellite would be locked down tighter than Fort Knox, right? Nope. Here's why satellites are often shockingly easy to hack:

- **Outdated Tech** – Some satellites still run on 30+ year-old firmware with no encryption. If it worked in the '90s, why change it? (Answer: Because hackers exist.)
- **Long Lifespan** – Unlike computers that get upgraded every few years, satellites are designed to last 10-20 years or more. Security patches? Good luck updating something in orbit.
- **Weak Encryption (or None at All)** – Many satellite signals are still sent in plaintext, making them easy to intercept.
- **Exposed Ground Stations** – Many satellite control centers use internet-connected software, making them vulnerable to remote exploits and phishing attacks.
- **Trust in Signal Integrity** – Most satellite-based systems (GPS, for example) assume whatever data they receive is legitimate, making spoofing attacks extremely effective.

If you've ever wondered how hackers falsify GPS coordinates, intercept satellite internet, or even hijack satellite controls, it all comes down to bad security practices and outdated systems.

Real-World Satellite Hacks: Yes, It's Already Happened

If you think space cybersecurity is just a theoretical problem, think again. Here are some real-world incidents that prove just how vulnerable satellite systems are:

- **Chinese Hackers Breached U.S. Satellites (2007-2008)** – Hackers linked to China gained control of two U.S. satellites for several minutes by attacking a ground station.
- **Iranian Hackers Hijacked a Military Drone (2011)** – Iran intercepted GPS signals to trick a U.S. stealth drone into landing in their territory.

- **Satellite TV Signal Hijacking** – Hackers have repeatedly intercepted and replaced TV signals on satellites, broadcasting their own messages instead.

And let's not even get started on GPS spoofing attacks that have misled ships, aircraft, and entire military operations.

The Future of Space Security: Can We Fix It?

So, how do we stop satellites from becoming the next big cyberwarfare battleground? Here are a few things the industry is finally starting to implement:

- **End-to-End Encryption** – Encrypting all data from ground stations to satellites to prevent interception.
- **Quantum Encryption** – Using quantum key distribution (QKD) to create unbreakable encryption.
- **AI-Powered Intrusion Detection** – Implementing machine learning algorithms to detect and respond to cyberattacks in real time.
- **Regular Firmware Updates (Somehow)** – Finding ways to securely update satellite software without introducing new vulnerabilities.

But here's the reality: hackers are always one step ahead, and as long as satellites remain critical to global communications, navigation, and defense, they will always be prime targets for cyberattacks.

Final Thought: Hackers in Space? Yeah, It's Happening

The idea of hacking satellites once sounded like sci-fi, but today, it's a very real and very serious cybersecurity threat. Whether you're a hacker, a pentester, or just someone who thinks spoofing GPS sounds like a fun weekend project, one thing is clear—space is no longer just for astronauts. It's for hackers too.

So, if you're ready to explore the dark side of satellite security, buckle up. This is just the beginning. 🚀

1.2 Attack Surfaces in Satellite Communications and Infrastructure

Welcome to Space, Where Everything is Hackable!

If you thought hacking satellites would be some kind of impossible Hollywood-level, Mission Impossible, Tom Cruise-hanging-off-a-space-station kind of feat, let me stop you right there. It's easier than you think.

The reason? Satellites weren't designed with cybersecurity in mind. In the early days of space tech, the biggest concerns were keeping things running and not accidentally dropping a multi-billion-dollar satellite into the ocean. Security was an afterthought—if it was even a thought at all. Fast forward to today, and we're still dealing with ancient security flaws, unpatched vulnerabilities, and signals that practically invite eavesdroppers.

Satellite systems are massive, complex networks with numerous attack surfaces—some in space, some on the ground, and some floating somewhere in the middle, just waiting for the right hacker to come along. So, let's break down where the cracks are and how attackers can slip through them.

1. The Space-Based Attack Surfaces: Hacking the Floating Targets

Satellites may be miles above Earth, but that doesn't mean they're out of a hacker's reach. Far from it. There are several ways an attacker can intercept, manipulate, or even hijack a satellite while it's floating up there, blissfully unaware of the digital chaos unfolding below.

1.1 Uplink and Downlink Attacks

Satellites rely on radio frequency (RF) communications to send and receive data. Unfortunately, many of these signals are completely unencrypted, making them ripe for interception.

- **Eavesdropping**: Hackers with the right equipment (like a Software-Defined Radio) can simply listen in on unencrypted satellite transmissions. If governments and corporations are transmitting sensitive data in the clear, guess what? It's fair game.
- **Man-in-the-Middle (MITM) Attacks**: Attackers can intercept, modify, and retransmit signals between a ground station and a satellite, feeding false data to unsuspecting users.
- **Signal Replay Attacks**: Some systems are so outdated that they don't even verify whether a command is coming from an authorized source. Hackers can record legitimate satellite commands and replay them later to trigger actions like orbital adjustments or data dumps.

1.2 GPS and GNSS Spoofing

Want to make a ship think it's in the middle of the Atlantic when it's actually near the coast of Somalia? Or trick a drone into flying into restricted airspace? That's what GPS spoofing does.

- GPS satellites trust whatever signals they receive, which makes them highly vulnerable to spoofing attacks where hackers create fake signals that override real GPS data.
- In 2019, GPS spoofing was suspected in massive maritime incidents, where ships mysteriously started reporting false locations hundreds of miles away from their actual positions.

1.3 Jamming Attacks

If intercepting and spoofing isn't your style, there's always the brute-force method: jamming the signal altogether.

- RF jamming can disrupt satellite communications, making it impossible for a target to receive or send data.
- GPS jamming has been used in military operations to confuse enemy forces by disabling navigation systems.
- Some commercial airlines have even experienced GPS signal loss due to accidental (or intentional) jamming, proving just how easy it is to cause large-scale disruptions.

2. Ground-Based Attack Surfaces: The Real Weak Links

While hacking an orbiting satellite sounds cool, most successful attacks actually start on the ground. Ground stations, relay networks, and user endpoints are often easier to compromise than the satellite itself. Here's how:

2.1 Hacking Ground Stations

Ground stations are the control centers for satellites, responsible for sending commands, receiving data, and managing software updates. If a hacker can breach a ground station, they effectively control the satellite.

- **Default Credentials and Poor Security Practices**: Believe it or not, some ground station systems still use default usernames and passwords. (Because apparently, "admin/admin" is still a thing in space.)
- **Internet-Exposed Systems**: Many satellite control systems are connected to the internet, sometimes without proper firewalls, making them vulnerable to remote attacks and malware infections.
- **Phishing and Social Engineering**: Why break in when you can just ask nicely? Spear-phishing attacks against ground station employees can lead to stolen credentials and unauthorized access.

2.2 Exploiting Satellite IoT Devices

Space IoT is growing fast, with small, internet-connected devices helping with satellite monitoring, data collection, and communication relays. But here's the problem: most IoT devices are insecure as hell.

- **Unpatched Firmware**: Attackers can exploit vulnerabilities in IoT firmware to gain access to satellite systems.
- **Weak Authentication**: If an IoT device is communicating with a satellite but lacks proper authentication mechanisms, hackers can spoof the device and send malicious commands.

2.3 Cloud-Based Satellite Control Systems

Many modern satellites are managed through cloud platforms, allowing operators to send commands remotely via APIs and web-based dashboards. Convenient? Yes. Secure? Not always.

- **Poor API Security**: If an attacker gains access to a cloud-based satellite control API, they can send rogue commands to disrupt operations.
- **Credential Stuffing Attacks**: Since some cloud-based control systems rely on web logins, attackers can use stolen credentials from data breaches to gain unauthorized access.

3. Relay and Data Interception Attacks: Messing with the Middlemen

Satellites don't always communicate directly with ground stations—they often use relay satellites and network gateways to pass data between different parts of the world. This creates additional attack surfaces:

- **Data Interception via Relay Satellites**: If a hacker can position themselves between a relay and a ground station, they can intercept and modify data in transit.
- **Exploiting Weak Encryption in Data Links**: Some relay networks still use outdated or weak encryption standards, making them vulnerable to brute-force decryption or traffic analysis attacks.

Final Thought: Space is Just Another Battlefield

At the end of the day, satellites are just computers in space—and computers can be hacked. The difference? When a system gets hacked on Earth, you can just unplug it and reboot. When it happens in space? Well... good luck.

Attack surfaces in satellite infrastructure are everywhere—from unsecured radio signals to hijackable ground stations. The more satellites we launch, the bigger the attack surface grows.

So, if you've ever dreamed of hacking a satellite (for ethical reasons, of course), now's the time to learn. Because if history has taught us anything, when something is connected, it can be exploited. And satellites? They're more connected than ever. 🚀

1.3 Key Threats: Jamming, Spoofing, Hijacking, and Data Interception

Houston, We Have a Cybersecurity Problem

So, you want to hack a satellite? Well, grab your tinfoil hat, fire up your SDR (Software-Defined Radio), and welcome to the wild west of space cybersecurity.

Satellites weren't built with cyber threats in mind, but attackers sure as hell figured out how to mess with them. Jamming, spoofing, hijacking, and data interception—these are the four horsemen of satellite insecurity, and they've been wreaking havoc for years.

Governments use them for military operations, hackers exploit them for espionage, and sometimes, bored hobbyists just want to see if they can mess with signals from space (spoiler: they can). So, let's break down these threats, see how they work, and why they're way too easy to pull off.

1. Jamming: The Art of Screaming Loudly in Space

Imagine you're at a rock concert, trying to talk to your friend, but the speakers are blasting at 130 decibels. That's what jamming does—it drowns out legitimate satellite signals with noise so nothing gets through.

How Jamming Works

Jamming is one of the simplest and most effective attacks against satellites. It involves blasting a stronger signal on the same frequency as the target satellite transmission, effectively making communication impossible.

Uplink Jamming: The attacker blocks signals being sent to the satellite, preventing commands from reaching it.

Downlink Jamming: The attacker disrupts signals coming from the satellite, affecting users on Earth.

Real-World Jamming Attacks

In 2012, Iran jammed BBC satellite broadcasts, disrupting news reports they didn't like.

North Korea has jammed GPS signals multiple times, interfering with navigation in South Korea.

In 2022, during the Russia-Ukraine conflict, Viasat's satellite network was jammed, taking down internet services for thousands of users.

Defense Against Jamming

Frequency hopping: Rapidly switching frequencies makes it harder for attackers to jam signals.

Directional antennas: These focus signals in a tight beam, reducing interference from other sources.

Encrypted signals: While encryption doesn't prevent jamming, it ensures that even if a signal is intercepted, it remains unreadable.

2. Spoofing: The Art of Lying to Satellites

If jamming is like screaming at someone so they can't hear anything, spoofing is like impersonating their best friend and feeding them bad information.

How Spoofing Works

Spoofing involves sending fake signals that a satellite or receiver mistakenly trusts as real. This can be used to:

Fake GPS locations (tricking ships, drones, or even entire military units).

Inject false data into a satellite system.

Manipulate satellite-controlled devices on Earth.

Real-World Spoofing Attacks

In 2013, university researchers spoofed a yacht's GPS, making it veer off course without the crew realizing.

China and Russia have been accused of GPS spoofing, redirecting ships and aircraft away from restricted areas.

In 2019, over 20 ships in the Black Sea mysteriously showed false GPS locations, likely due to spoofing.

Defense Against Spoofing

Multi-frequency GPS: Modern GNSS receivers use multiple signals, making it harder to spoof all of them.

Encrypted GPS signals: Some military GPS signals use encryption, making them resistant to spoofing.

AI-based anomaly detection: Machine learning can detect unusual patterns in navigation data.

3. Hijacking: When Hackers Take the Wheel

Jamming and spoofing are annoying. Hijacking is terrifying. This is when an attacker takes full control of a satellite—potentially redirecting it, shutting it down, or even using it for espionage.

How Hijacking Works

Many satellites still use weak authentication or default credentials, meaning an attacker with the right access can issue unauthorized commands.

Some satellite control stations are connected to the internet (bad idea), making them vulnerable to hacking.

Once inside, an attacker can manipulate software, disrupt services, or even disable a satellite entirely.

Real-World Hijacking Attacks

In 1999, hackers took control of a UK military satellite, demanding ransom for its return.

Brazilian hackers hijacked military satellites in the 2000s to run illegal radio communications.

China allegedly attempted to gain control of U.S. satellites multiple times using cyber techniques.

Defense Against Hijacking

Strong authentication: Using multi-factor authentication and cryptographic keys can prevent unauthorized access.

Segmented networks: Keeping satellite control networks isolated from the internet reduces attack risks.

Regular security audits: Many satellite systems run on outdated software—updating and patching vulnerabilities is critical.

4. Data Interception: Eavesdropping from Space

What if you don't want to jam, spoof, or hijack? Maybe you just want to sit back, relax, and listen in on all the juicy satellite data. Welcome to data interception.

How Data Interception Works

Many satellites still transmit data in the clear—no encryption, no security, just open signals waiting to be intercepted.

Attackers can use cheap SDR kits (under $300) to capture unencrypted transmissions.

Military, government, and corporate communications can be intercepted, analyzed, and even manipulated.

Real-World Data Interception Attacks

Amateur radio enthusiasts have intercepted space shuttle communications.

Sensitive military transmissions have been picked up by foreign intelligence agencies.

Hackers have extracted unencrypted satellite internet traffic, reading emails and messages in real-time.

Defense Against Data Interception

Encryption: Using strong encryption for all satellite communications makes intercepted data useless.

Frequency-hopping spread spectrum (FHSS): This technique switches frequencies rapidly, making interception harder.

Directional antennas: Reducing signal leakage makes it harder for attackers to capture data.

Final Thought: Welcome to the War Zone

If you thought hacking satellites was just sci-fi nonsense, think again. The threats are real, active, and growing. From jamming and spoofing to full-blown hijacking, space has become the new battleground for cyber warfare.

And the worst part? Many satellite systems are still ridiculously insecure.

Governments, militaries, corporations, and even cybercriminals are actively exploiting these vulnerabilities. Whether it's manipulating GPS data, shutting down communications, or spying on sensitive transmissions, space hacking is here, and it's not going away.

So next time you look up at the night sky, just remember—someone, somewhere, might be hacking a satellite at that very moment. 🚀

1.4 Legal and Ethical Considerations in Satellite Hacking (FCC, ITU, Outer Space Treaty)

So, You Want to Hack a Satellite? Let's Talk About Prison First.

Ah, satellite hacking. It sounds like the ultimate cyberpunk dream—hijacking signals from space, bypassing government-controlled communications, maybe even redirecting a weather satellite just to mess with your local forecast. But before you grab your SDR and start blasting signals into the void, let's talk about the legal (a.k.a. "how to avoid jail") and ethical (a.k.a. "should you even do this?") sides of satellite security research.

Because here's the deal—space may be infinite, but laws and international regulations are very real. The moment you start poking at a satellite, you're potentially violating a dozen different laws, treaties, and regulations. Governments don't take too kindly to random people messing with billion-dollar space assets. So, unless you enjoy the idea of the FBI (or worse, a nation-state intelligence agency) knocking on your door, let's break down what's legal, what's not, and what ethical hacking looks like in space.

The Big Three: FCC, ITU, and the Outer Space Treaty

Satellite communications aren't just floating around waiting for someone to hack them— they're regulated by major international and national organizations. These are the big ones you need to know:

Federal Communications Commission (FCC) – If you're in the U.S., the FCC is the biggest regulatory body for all things radio and satellite-related. They manage frequency allocations and licensing.

International Telecommunication Union (ITU) – This UN agency regulates global satellite communications, frequency spectrum, and orbital slots. If you mess with satellite signals, you're violating international law.

The Outer Space Treaty (OST, 1967) – The granddaddy of space law, signed by 113 countries, including the U.S., Russia, and China. It sets broad rules for space operations, including banning harmful interference with satellites.

Now, let's dig into the do's and don'ts of satellite hacking under these laws.

1. The FCC: The "We'll Find You" Agency

The FCC has a lot of power, and if you operate in the U.S., violating their rules can result in hefty fines, equipment seizures, and even prison time.

What's Illegal?

Unauthorized transmission on satellite frequencies – Broadcasting on licensed satellite bands without permission? That's a big no-no.

Jamming satellite signals – Even if you're "just testing," you could disrupt emergency or military communications.

Modifying commercial satellite services – Interfering with services like Starlink, Inmarsat, or Iridium is a fast track to legal trouble.

What's Legal?

Passive listening – In most cases, receiving unencrypted signals isn't illegal. However, decoding encrypted data is illegal, even if you don't transmit anything.

Licensed research – If you have FCC authorization, you can legally conduct satellite security research in a controlled environment.

◆ FCC Penalty Example:

In 2018, a U.S. company was fined $2.8 million for launching and operating unauthorized satellites. If they're willing to fine corporations, imagine what they'll do to a random hacker.

2. The ITU: The International Frequency Police

The International Telecommunication Union (ITU) is a UN agency that controls the global radio frequency spectrum. It ensures that satellite signals don't interfere with each other and that all space-faring nations follow the rules.

What's Illegal?

Interfering with international satellite signals – The ITU coordinates frequency use worldwide. If you jam or spoof satellite signals across borders, you're violating international law.

Unauthorized use of satellite bandwidth – Many satellites lease bandwidth to governments and companies. Using it without permission is a huge violation.

What's Legal?

Monitoring ITU-registered satellite signals – The ITU publishes frequency allocations, and listening to unencrypted transmissions for research is generally allowed.

Reporting vulnerabilities responsibly – Ethical hackers who discover security flaws should report them through coordinated disclosure programs to satellite operators.

◆ Real-World Example:

In 2015, pirates hijacked a satellite to broadcast illegal TV channels. They were eventually tracked and shut down using ITU-coordinated efforts.

3. The Outer Space Treaty: The Oldest Space Law in the Books

Signed in 1967, the Outer Space Treaty (OST) is the foundation of international space law. It covers everything from military activities in space to the legal status of celestial bodies.

What's Illegal?

Causing "harmful interference" with satellites – This means jamming, spoofing, hijacking, or interfering with a satellite's normal function.

Using space for hostile activities – Cyberattacks on satellites are often seen as acts of war, and some countries may retaliate accordingly.

What's Legal?

Defensive cybersecurity research – As long as you don't interfere with live satellites, studying security flaws in test environments is acceptable.

Building open-source security tools – Many cybersecurity experts develop legal tools to help strengthen satellite security.

◆ **Real-World Case:**

During the Russia-Ukraine war, satellite cyberattacks were linked to state-sponsored hackers. These incidents blurred the line between cybercrime and military action, showing how serious space cybersecurity has become.

Ethical Hacking in Space: The Right Way to Do It

Legal constraints aside, let's talk ethics. Just because something is technically possible doesn't mean you should do it. Ethical hacking follows these principles:

✓ **Do no harm** – Security research should never disrupt actual satellite operations.
✓ **Obtain permission** – If you want to test satellite vulnerabilities, get authorization from the satellite operator.
✓ **Use responsible disclosure** – If you find a flaw, report it privately to the right people instead of exploiting it.
✓ **Protect critical infrastructure** – Satellites control navigation, communications, military operations, and global internet—messing with them can have real-world consequences.

Final Thought: Don't Be the Guy Who Gets Banned from Space

Look, I get it. Satellite hacking is cool, and the idea of playing around with signals from orbit sounds like something out of a spy movie. But unless you want to end up on an international watchlist, you need to know the laws.

Remember: ethical hackers work to strengthen security, not exploit it. There's plenty of legal, responsible research to do in satellite security, from finding vulnerabilities to developing better encryption methods.

So, before you start messing with satellite signals, ask yourself: Do I want to be a security researcher, or do I want to spend my life avoiding extradition? 🚀

1.5 Setting Up a Research Lab for Satellite Security Testing

So You Want to Hack Satellites? Time to Build a Lab!

Alright, so you've read about the attack surfaces, learned the legal do's and don'ts, and now you're itching to dive into satellite security testing. But before you start pointing your SDR at the sky like some kind of cyberpunk wizard, you need a proper lab setup. Because let's be real—hacking satellites from your living room with a tin foil hat isn't exactly the best approach.

A good research lab isn't just about having the latest tools and gadgets; it's about understanding the environment you're working with, following legal guidelines, and building a controlled space to test satellite vulnerabilities without violating international treaties (because no one wants to explain to the FBI why they accidentally jammed a weather satellite).

Let's walk through how to set up a proper, ethical, and effective satellite security testing lab.

1. Understanding the Scope of Your Lab

Before you start buying hardware and setting up antennas, ask yourself: What are you actually trying to test?

A satellite security lab can focus on multiple areas:

Passive signal analysis – Monitoring and decoding unencrypted satellite communications.

Protocol research – Studying the security of satellite communication protocols like CCSDS, DVB-S, and GNSS.

Software and firmware analysis – Reverse engineering satellite firmware and ground station software.

Red teaming simulations – Ethical hacking exercises to test vulnerabilities in satellite networks (with permission, of course).

Each area requires different tools and techniques, so defining your scope helps you invest in the right equipment.

2. Essential Hardware for Your Lab

Now, let's talk gear. You don't need a NASA-sized budget to get started, but you do need the right tools:

✓ Software-Defined Radios (SDRs)

HackRF One – A great entry-level SDR for general RF research.

BladeRF – A step up for more advanced satellite signal analysis.

USRP B210 – High-performance SDR, ideal for working with a broad range of frequencies.

✓ Antennas

Parabolic Dish Antenna – Essential for receiving signals from geostationary satellites.

Yagi Antenna – Great for tracking low-earth orbit (LEO) satellites.

Helical Antenna – Used for circularly polarized satellite signals.

✓ Ground Station Equipment

GNSS Receiver – For studying GPS and GNSS spoofing techniques.

Low-Noise Block Downconverter (LNB) – Helps convert satellite signals to a usable frequency.

Rotator System – Automatically tracks moving satellites in orbit.

✓ Computing and Processing Power

A powerful laptop or desktop – Preferably with a high-performance GPU for signal processing.

Raspberry Pi / Jetson Nano – Great for portable satellite signal analysis.

3. Software and Tools for Satellite Hacking

A lab is only as good as the tools you use. Here are some essential software programs for satellite security testing:

✓ Signal Processing and SDR Tools

GNU Radio – Open-source software for working with SDR data.

SDR# (SDRSharp) – A user-friendly tool for analyzing RF signals.

GQRX – A simple but powerful SDR receiver application.

✓ Satellite Tracking and Recon Tools

GPredict – Real-time satellite tracking software.

SatNOGS – A global open-source satellite ground station network.

TLE Trackers – Tools that use Two-Line Element (TLE) data to predict satellite orbits.

✓ Protocol Analysis and Security Tools

Wireshark – Essential for analyzing network packets in satellite communications.

Scapy – Python-based packet manipulation tool.

CCSDS Space Packet Decoder – Used for analyzing space communication protocols.

4. Setting Up a Legal and Ethical Testing Environment

Before you start experimenting, make sure your lab setup follows legal and ethical best practices:

✓ Passive Listening is Legal (Mostly)

Receiving unencrypted satellite signals is usually allowed.

However, decrypting encrypted signals is illegal unless you have permission.

✓ No Unauthorized Transmissions

Broadcasting on satellite frequencies without a license is a serious offense.

Always use a controlled RF environment or simulation tools when testing.

✓ Use Simulations Whenever Possible

Instead of testing on live satellites, use software-defined satellite simulators to create a virtual testbed.

Tools like GNU Radio and MATLAB can simulate satellite communication scenarios.

5. Creating a Simulated Satellite Network for Testing

A realistic but controlled testing environment is key to ethical satellite security research. Here's how to set up a simulated satellite network:

Step 1: Build a Virtual Satellite System

Use tools like OpenSatKit and CubeSatSim to simulate a working satellite.

Create virtual ground stations using SDR-based receivers.

Step 2: Emulate Satellite Communications

Configure DVB-S or CCSDS protocols for simulated data transmission.

Set up a mock GPS/GNSS environment to study spoofing techniques legally.

Step 3: Test Security Defenses

Implement encryption and authentication measures in the simulation.

Conduct penetration tests to identify weaknesses.

This setup lets you practice real-world attack and defense techniques without violating any laws.

6. Joining the Global Satellite Security Community

Cybersecurity is a team sport, and the satellite security world is no different. If you're serious about this field, connect with other researchers:

✓ Online Communities and Forums

SatNOGS Community – Open-source satellite ground station network.

RTL-SDR Forum – Great place to discuss SDR and satellite hacking.

DEF CON Aerospace Village – Security research focused on satellites and space systems.

✓ Capture the Flag (CTF) and Hacking Challenges

Hack-A-Sat – A satellite hacking competition hosted by the U.S. Air Force.

CyberSkyline Space Security Challenges – Hands-on satellite cybersecurity challenges.

Final Thought: Build a Lab, Not a Lawsuit

Setting up a satellite security lab is an exciting and rewarding step into the world of space cybersecurity. But remember—responsible research is key. You don't want to wake up one day with a government agency asking why your SDR was interfering with military satellites.

So go forth, build your lab, experiment responsibly, and most importantly—don't be the guy who accidentally jams the International Space Station's comms. 🚀

Chapter 2: Understanding Satellite Architectures and Protocols

Ever tried fixing your Wi-Fi and realized you barely understand how your own router works? Now imagine that router is moving at 17,500 mph, orbiting the Earth, and costing a few hundred million dollars. Yeah, things get complicated fast. But don't worry—we're here to break it all down in plain English. By the time you're done with this chapter, you'll be able to tell your friends the difference between a ground station and a relay satellite without sounding like you just made it up.

In this chapter, we'll dissect the components of a satellite system, covering everything from ground stations and payloads to the different frequency bands used in space communication. We'll also introduce key protocols like CCSDS, DVB-S, and Iridium, highlighting how data is transmitted, encrypted, and (unfortunately) sometimes intercepted. This foundational knowledge is essential for understanding how cyberattacks can target space-based systems.

2.1 Components of a Satellite System (Ground Stations, Relays, Payloads)

Satellites: Not Just Fancy Space Junk!

Ever looked up at the night sky and thought, "I wonder how many satellites are up there spying on me?" Well, the answer is: a lot. But before you start waving at them (or wearing a tinfoil hat), let's break down how these satellites actually work.

A satellite isn't just a floating hunk of metal drifting through space—it's part of a massive interconnected system. It's like the ultimate long-distance relationship: satellites need ground stations to talk to, relays to pass messages, and payloads to do their actual jobs.

If one of these components fails, the whole system can fall apart. Imagine trying to send a text, but your phone, Wi-Fi, and carrier network all stop working at the same time. Yeah, that's how crucial these components are. So, let's break them down and see what makes them tick.

1. Ground Stations: The Brains of the Operation

Think of ground stations as Mission Control for satellites. Without them, satellites would just be silent, lonely hunks of metal floating in space, unsure of what to do next.

What Do Ground Stations Do?

Send Commands: "Hey satellite, take this picture of Antarctica."

Receive Data: "Here's your picture of Antarctica."

Monitor Health: "Hey satellite, are you feeling okay?"

Manage Orbit Adjustments: "Uh-oh, you're drifting. Let's fix that."

Components of a Ground Station:

Antennas – Giant dishes or arrays that communicate with satellites.

RF Transceivers – Convert signals to usable data.

Mission Control Software – The interface used to send commands and receive telemetry.

Secure Communication Links – Because you don't want random hackers sending commands to your satellites (looking at you, space pirates).

Ground stations aren't just in one location—they're spread across the globe to maintain continuous contact with satellites. The Deep Space Network (DSN), for example, has stations in California, Spain, and Australia to ensure NASA's deep-space probes never go silent.

And yes, some ground stations have been hacked before. Because why break into a bank when you can control a satellite instead?

2. Relays: The Space Mailmen

Satellites don't always talk directly to Earth. Sometimes they use relay satellites—essentially cosmic mail couriers that pass messages between the satellite and ground stations.

Why Are Relays Important?

Extends Coverage – Some satellites (especially in deep space) can't always connect to Earth, so relays help.

Reduces Communication Delays – Instead of waiting for a satellite to be in range of a ground station, relays keep the data flowing.

Used for Military & Commercial Ops – Systems like the Tracking and Data Relay Satellite System (TDRSS) handle mission-critical data for NASA and defense agencies.

Without relays, real-time satellite communication would be a nightmare. Imagine trying to stream Netflix, but your Wi-Fi only works for ten minutes every few hours. Yeah, not fun.

3. Payloads: The Reason Satellites Exist

Satellites aren't just up there for decoration—they all have a mission, and that mission is handled by the payload.

What is a Payload?

The payload is the business end of a satellite. It's what makes a satellite useful. Everything else (power, propulsion, communication) exists just to keep the payload operational.

Common Types of Payloads:

Imaging Systems – Cameras for Earth observation, spy satellites, and weather tracking.

Communication Modules – Transmit TV, radio, and internet signals (hello, Starlink).

Scientific Instruments – Measure cosmic radiation, scan planets, or study space weather.

Navigation Systems – GPS satellites help your phone tell you to take that wrong turn.

Defense and Military Payloads – Because governments like to keep an eye on each other.

Satellites can have multiple payloads, too. Some weather satellites double as communication relays, while military satellites might combine navigation, communication, and surveillance into one high-tech package.

The Symbiotic Relationship: How It All Works Together

Think of the entire satellite system like an orchestra:

Ground Stations are the conductors, giving instructions.

Satellites and Relays are the musicians, carrying the tune.

Payloads are the instruments, making the music happen.

If any one of these components fails, the entire system breaks down. A broken relay means lost data. A non-functional payload means a useless satellite taking up space. And if a ground station goes offline? Well, let's just say that satellite might be lost in space forever.

Final Thoughts: Don't Call it "Just a Satellite"

Next time you hear someone say, "It's just a satellite", remind them that a satellite is part of a complex, high-tech network of space-age wizardry that keeps our world running.

And if you're ever in doubt about how important satellites are, just turn off GPS, Wi-Fi, and satellite TV for a day and see how much you miss them. 😄

2.2 Satellite Communication Frequencies and Bands (L, S, C, X, Ku, Ka)

Radio Waves: The Cosmic Wi-Fi That Runs the Universe

You ever wonder how your GPS tells you exactly where you are (even though you have no idea how you got there)? Or how you can stream cat videos from space via satellite internet? The answer lies in the magic of radio waves—or, more accurately, in the different frequency bands that satellites use to communicate.

But let's be real: the world of satellite frequency bands can feel like a soup of random letters—L-band, S-band, C-band, X-band, Ku-band, Ka-band... It's like someone just went wild with the alphabet. But don't worry—I'll break it down for you in a way that won't make your brain melt.

So, buckle up. We're about to take a first-class tour through the electromagnetic spectrum, where satellites are basically giant cosmic routers.

What Are Satellite Frequency Bands?

A frequency band is just a range of radio frequencies used for communication. Different satellites use different bands based on what they need to do—some are good for long-distance signals, some are great for high-speed data, and others just like being complicated.

Satellite communication relies on specific bands of the radio frequency (RF) spectrum, ranging from 1 GHz to over 30 GHz. The choice of band depends on factors like:

✔ **Data rate needs** – Are we sending a simple weather report or streaming 4K video from space?
✔ **Atmospheric interference** – Rain, clouds, and even cosmic radiation can mess with certain frequencies.
✔ **Antenna size requirements** – Lower frequencies need big antennas, while higher frequencies work with smaller dishes.

Each band has unique characteristics that make it perfect for certain tasks. Let's break them down.

1. L-Band (1–2 GHz) – The Reliable Workhorse

◆ **Used for**: GPS, mobile satellite communication, aircraft navigation

L-band is the granddaddy of satellite communication—it's been around forever and refuses to die. It has long wavelengths, which means it can punch through bad weather, trees, and even some buildings like a champ.

✔ Pros:

Resistant to rain and atmospheric interference

Great for mobile applications (like GPS)

Works with small antennas

✗ Cons:

Slow data speeds – Not ideal for high-bandwidth applications

Limited spectrum availability

Real-world use case: Every time your GPS tells you to take a left turn into a lake, you can thank L-band satellites for that questionable advice.

2. S-Band (2–4 GHz) – The Space Nerd's Favorite

◆ Used for: Weather satellites, deep space communications, radar

S-band is like L-band's cooler, slightly faster cousin. It's commonly used for:

Weather monitoring satellites □□

Space-to-Earth communication (like talking to the International Space Station)

Military radars and missile tracking

✓ Pros:

Works well through rain and clouds

Still uses relatively small antennas

Reliable for telemetry and deep space probes

✗ Cons:

Limited bandwidth compared to higher frequencies

Not ideal for high-speed data transmission

Real-world use case: The Mars rovers send data back to Earth through S-band relays before it reaches NASA's Deep Space Network. So yeah, if you love pictures of Martian rocks, thank S-band.

3. C-Band (4–8 GHz) – The Old-School TV King

◆ **Used for**: Satellite TV, long-distance communication, early internet satellites

C-band is like the satellite grandpa—it's been around forever and is still surprisingly useful. It's widely used in broadcasting, especially for transmitting TV signals across continents.

✅ Pros:

Highly reliable (used by major TV networks)

Not affected by rain or bad weather

Good for long-range communication

✖ Cons:

Requires large dish antennas (you've probably seen those giant satellite dishes)

Limited bandwidth compared to newer bands

Real-world use case: If you ever watched a live sports broadcast from another country, there's a good chance the signal traveled via C-band satellites.

4. X-Band (8–12 GHz) – The Military's Favorite Playground

◆ **Used for**: Military satellite communications, radars, secret government stuff 🚀

X-band is like the classified VIP section of satellite communication. It's mainly reserved for military and government use. You won't find Netflix streaming on X-band—unless the government is hiding something from us. 👀

✅ Pros:

Works well in adverse weather conditions

Highly secure (encrypted military communications)

Ideal for radar and defense systems

✘ Cons:

Not available for public use

Requires specialized receivers and equipment

Real-world use case: Ever wonder how the military communicates with stealth bombers or spy satellites? Yep, X-band is doing the heavy lifting.

5. Ku-Band (12–18 GHz) – The Satellite Internet Superhighway

◆ **Used for**: Satellite TV, broadband internet (Starlink, VSAT)

Ku-band is the workhorse of modern satellite communication. If you've ever used satellite internet on a plane, you were likely connected to a Ku-band satellite.

✓ Pros:

Smaller antennas (which is why planes and ships love it)

High-speed data transmission

Perfect for live broadcasting and broadband internet

✘ Cons:

Easily affected by rain and clouds (rain fade)

Higher interference risk compared to lower bands

Real-world use case: Starlink, Inmarsat, and other satellite internet providers use Ku-band for global broadband access.

6. Ka-Band (18–40 GHz) – The Future of Space Internet

◆ **Used for**: Ultra-fast satellite internet, high-resolution radar, deep space communications

Ka-band is the speed demon of satellite frequencies—it's used for next-gen broadband, 4K video streaming, and deep space missions.

✅ Pros:

Super high-speed internet 🚀

Supports ultra-HD streaming

Great for high-resolution imaging and radar

✖ Cons:

Highly sensitive to rain and atmospheric conditions

Requires very precise alignment of antennas

Real-world use case: NASA's Mars Reconnaissance Orbiter uses Ka-band to send high-resolution images of Mars back to Earth. Also, 5G satellite backhaul networks are starting to use Ka-band for ultra-fast data speeds.

Final Thoughts: Frequency Bands Matter More Than You Think

If satellite communication was a music festival, different bands would be playing different sets:

🎸 **L-Band** – Classic Rock (Reliable, never dies)
♪ **S-Band** – Jazz (Used for deep space comms)
📺 **C-Band** – Old-School Pop (TV, radio, broadcasting)
☐ **X-Band** – Military Metal (Top secret)
🚀 **Ku-Band** – EDM (Fast, modern, internet-driven)
🔊 **Ka-Band** – Future Bass (Ultra-fast data, 5G)

So next time you use GPS, stream a satellite video, or see a spy thriller where satellites track someone in real time, you'll know exactly what frequencies are at play. And yes, rain can actually kill your satellite internet, and now you know why. 😄

2.3 Space IoT Protocols: CCSDS, DVB-S, Iridium, Inmarsat, GNSS

Space IoT: Because Even Satellites Need to Speak the Same Language

Alright, let's get one thing straight: space isn't some lawless cyberpunk wasteland where satellites just scream radio signals into the void hoping something, somewhere, understands them. No, just like Earth's internet has TCP/IP, space has its own set of communication protocols—the secret sauce that lets satellites, ground stations, and spaceborne IoT devices talk to each other without losing their cosmic minds.

Think of these protocols as the WhatsApp, Zoom, and Morse code of space—but with way cooler names like CCSDS, DVB-S, Iridium, Inmarsat, and GNSS. Each one has a different job, from beaming satellite TV to guiding missiles (hopefully for the right reasons) and keeping astronauts from getting lost in space.

So, grab your astronaut helmet (or just a strong cup of coffee), and let's dive into the protocols that make space IoT possible!

1. CCSDS (Consultative Committee for Space Data Systems) – The NASA of Protocols

If you've ever watched a rocket launch and wondered, "How do they send all that data from space without it turning into an intergalactic game of telephone?"—the answer is CCSDS.

CCSDS is a global standard used by space agencies like NASA, ESA, and JAXA to ensure satellites, rovers, and deep-space probes can exchange data reliably. It's essentially the ISO for space communications, defining how data should be formatted, transmitted, and even protected from cosmic interference.

✅ **Why It Matters:**

Standardized protocols mean agencies can share data without reinventing the wheel.

Supports error correction, because losing a rover's signal on Mars is not an option.

Used for deep-space missions, space telescopes, and interplanetary exploration.

🚀 **Real-World Example**: When the Perseverance Rover sends HD selfies from Mars, it follows CCSDS standards to make sure NASA actually gets the pics.

2. DVB-S (Digital Video Broadcasting - Satellite) – The Netflix of Space

DVB-S is the protocol that lets satellites beam video, internet, and data across the globe. If you've ever used a satellite TV service, streamed an onboard airplane movie, or connected to the internet in the middle of nowhere, you've used DVB-S.

It's optimized for high-bandwidth, one-way broadcasts, making it perfect for TV networks, weather satellites, and even military transmissions.

✅ **Why It Matters:**

Allows high-speed, long-range data transmission (like satellite internet).

Used for global news broadcasts, emergency alerts, and even remote education.

Supports multicast, so one satellite can send data to millions of receivers at once.

📡 **Real-World Example**: Your satellite TV subscription? DVB-S. Those giant satellite dishes at news stations? DVB-S. SpaceX's Starlink (while slightly different)? Also inspired by DVB-like tech.

3. Iridium – The Mobile Network for Space and Beyond

Imagine if your cell phone worked anywhere on Earth, from the middle of the Sahara to Antarctica to floating on a boat in the Pacific. That's Iridium—a satellite network designed to provide global voice and data coverage.

It operates using 66 low-Earth orbit (LEO) satellites, which act like cell towers in space, bouncing signals across the planet. Unlike traditional satellites, Iridium's system doesn't rely on ground stations—it communicates satellite-to-satellite before reaching your device.

✅ Why It Matters:

Offers truly global coverage, even in the most remote locations.

Used by militaries, rescue teams, maritime fleets, and even astronauts.

Works for satellite phones, emergency beacons, and IoT sensors.

📡 **Real-World Example**: When Elon Musk tweets from the middle of the ocean, he's probably using an Iridium satellite phone.

4. Inmarsat – The Swiss Army Knife of Satellite Communication

If Iridium is the cell phone network of space, then Inmarsat is the high-speed internet provider. Originally designed for maritime and aviation communication, Inmarsat has evolved into a multi-purpose network for internet, emergency response, and even military operations.

Unlike Iridium's LEO satellites, Inmarsat operates in geostationary orbit (GEO), meaning its satellites stay fixed over specific parts of the Earth. This makes it ideal for stable, high-bandwidth connections.

✅ Why It Matters:

Provides high-speed broadband to ships, planes, and remote regions.

Supports aviation safety systems, military comms, and disaster recovery.

Works for industrial IoT applications, like oil rigs and remote mining operations.

📡 **Real-World Example**: When an airplane gets Wi-Fi at 35,000 feet, there's a good chance it's connected to an Inmarsat satellite.

5. GNSS (Global Navigation Satellite System) – The Space Compass

Ever used Google Maps to find a pizza place? Congratulations, you've used GNSS, the backbone of global navigation.

GNSS is an umbrella term for all global positioning systems, including:

GPS (USA)

Galileo (Europe)

GLONASS (Russia)

BeiDou (China)

Each system uses a network of orbiting satellites that send timing signals to receivers (like your phone), allowing them to calculate precise locations.

✅ Why It Matters:

Powers everything from Uber rides to missile guidance systems.

Supports autonomous vehicles, agriculture, and emergency response.

Used in scientific research, weather forecasting, and space navigation.

📡 **Real-World Example**: Every time your GPS tells you to take an unnecessary U-turn, that's GNSS doing its thing (or messing with you).

Final Thoughts: Space IoT Needs a Common Language

Without standardized protocols, space communication would be absolute chaos—a cosmic version of trying to text your friend from an iPhone to an ancient flip phone.

Luckily, CCSDS, DVB-S, Iridium, Inmarsat, and GNSS ensure that satellites, ground stations, and IoT devices can all speak the same language, whether they're streaming TV, guiding missiles, or keeping astronauts alive.

And if you ever find yourself stranded in space, just remember: at least one of these protocols is probably trying to save your life. 🚀

2.4 Data Transmission in Space: Encryption and Compression Methods

Lost in Space? Encrypt It Before the Aliens Read It!

Alright, imagine you're an astronaut sending a private text message to Earth:

"Houston, I left my snacks on the ISS. Send Doritos on the next resupply, over."

Now, imagine that every satellite, rogue hacker, and possibly a bored alien in a distant galaxy can eavesdrop on that message. Not ideal, right? That's why encryption and compression are the Batman and Robin of space data transmission—protecting sensitive information while keeping it lightweight enough to survive the trip.

Because, let's be real—sending data across hundreds of thousands of kilometers is already hard enough. Now add cosmic radiation, signal degradation, and hackers who think space is their new playground, and you'll see why encryption and compression are absolute lifesavers.

Let's break down how space agencies and satellite companies keep their data secure, small, and speedy—without making our internet lag like it's 1999.

1. The Challenge of Space Data Transmission

Unlike sending a text or watching cat videos on YouTube, sending data from space isn't exactly plug-and-play. It faces several major challenges, including:

Long Distances – Data has to travel millions of kilometers (for deep-space missions) with a high risk of signal degradation.

Limited Bandwidth – Space communications have finite bandwidth, meaning we can't just send giant uncompressed images or videos.

Interference & Noise – Cosmic radiation, solar flares, and Earth's atmosphere can corrupt or distort signals.

Security Risks – Without strong encryption, satellites could be hijacked, spoofed, or intercepted by cybercriminals or hostile nations.

To deal with these issues, satellites use a combination of encryption for security and compression for efficiency—ensuring data stays safe and doesn't clog up the limited space pipelines.

2. Encryption: Keeping Space Data Safe from Hackers & Eavesdroppers

Think of encryption as the secret code that protects messages from being read by anyone who isn't supposed to. In space, encryption is even more critical because satellite signals can be intercepted by:

✅ Cybercriminals looking for sensitive military or financial data

✅ Nation-state hackers trying to gain an intelligence advantage

✅ Space pirates (okay, not yet, but give it time!)

To prevent unauthorized access, satellites use three major encryption techniques:

A. End-to-End Encryption (E2EE) – Locking Down Data from Start to Finish

With E2EE, data is encrypted before it even leaves the satellite and stays encrypted until it reaches the ground station. This ensures that even if an attacker intercepts the signal, they'll only see gibberish instead of valuable information.

☐ **Example:**

A spy satellite sends encrypted images of a military base to a command center. Even if a third party intercepts the transmission, they can't decrypt it without the proper keys.

B. AES (Advanced Encryption Standard) – The Gold Standard in Encryption

Most modern satellites use AES-256, a military-grade encryption standard that's so secure it would take a supercomputer millions of years to crack. It's the same encryption used by banks, governments, and your phone's Face ID system.

☐ **Example:**

When astronauts on the International Space Station send sensitive medical data, it's encrypted using AES to prevent interception by adversaries.

C. Quantum Encryption – The Future of Unbreakable Security

With the rise of quantum computing, traditional encryption might become hackable in the future. That's why space agencies are now exploring quantum encryption, where data is protected by the laws of quantum mechanics.

☐ **Example:**

China's Micius satellite has successfully tested quantum key distribution (QKD), proving that future space networks could be 100% hack-proof.

3. Compression: Sending More Data with Less Bandwidth

Now that we've locked down security, let's talk about efficiency.

Remember the 56K dial-up modem days, when downloading a single image took a full minute? That's what space transmission would feel like without compression.

Since bandwidth is precious in space, data must be compressed before transmission. Compression reduces file sizes without losing too much quality, allowing more information to be sent using the same limited bandwidth.

There are two types of compression:

A. Lossless Compression – Shrinking Data Without Losing a Single Bit

Lossless compression is like zipping a file—it reduces size without removing any data. It's ideal for:

✓ Scientific data from telescopes and probes

✓ Encrypted messages that must remain 100% accurate

☐ **Example:**

The Hubble Space Telescope compresses images losslessly to ensure that astronomers get exact, unaltered scientific data.

B. Lossy Compression – Trading Some Quality for Smaller Size

Lossy compression removes redundant or less important details, making files much smaller. It's used for:

✅ Streaming satellite TV (DVB-S)

✅ Satellite internet services like Starlink

✅ Weather images and terrain maps

⬜ **Example:**

Google Earth satellite images use lossy compression so you can load maps quickly, even if it means sacrificing some fine details.

4. Real-World Examples of Encryption & Compression in Action

🚀 NASA's Mars Rovers:

The Perseverance Rover encrypts critical command signals using AES-256 to prevent hacking.

It compresses HD images before sending them back to Earth to save bandwidth.

📡 Satellite Internet (Starlink, OneWeb, Inmarsat):

Uses end-to-end encryption to secure communications.

Compresses data streams to reduce latency and improve speeds.

⬜ Military & Government Satellites:

Use high-security encryption to prevent espionage.

Compress reconnaissance images before transmission to save precious bandwidth.

Final Thoughts: Encrypt It, Compress It, and Hope No One Hacks You

At the end of the day, space is a hostile place, and data must be protected from hackers, cosmic interference, and bad compression algorithms. That's why encryption and compression go hand in hand—one keeps data safe, and the other makes sure it actually gets delivered.

So, whether you're streaming satellite TV, guiding a rover on Mars, or just trying to send a "Happy Birthday" message to an astronaut, remember: Encrypt it. Compress it. And hope aliens don't have quantum decryption. 🚀

2.5 Hardening Satellite Communication Protocols Against Cyber Attacks

Welcome to Space: Where Hackers Don't Need Gravity to Cause Chaos

If you thought Wi-Fi hacking was bad, imagine someone intercepting a satellite signal from space and rerouting it to play Rick Astley's Never Gonna Give You Up across an entire nation's TV network. (Okay, that would be hilarious—but still, a serious problem.)

Satellite communications are essential for global connectivity, but they're also prime targets for cyberattacks. Unlike your home router, you can't just reset a satellite or install a quick firmware update—especially when it's orbiting 36,000 km above Earth. If a hacker exploits a vulnerability, they could:

✅ Jam satellite signals, cutting off internet, TV, and military communications.

✅ Spoof satellite transmissions, sending fake GPS data to ships, planes, or even self-driving cars.

✅ Hijack control systems, taking over satellites to disrupt national security.

So, how do we make satellite communication protocols hacker-proof? Let's dive into the best ways to harden satellite security and keep the cyber pirates from taking over our orbital highways.

1. Understanding the Weak Spots: Why Satellites Get Hacked

Before we lock down security, let's identify where satellites are most vulnerable:

☐ **Uplink & Downlink Interception** – Attackers can listen in on satellite communications or inject malicious data.

🦵 **Ground Station Exploits** – If hackers breach a ground station, they can control satellites remotely.

🕊 **Weak Encryption or No Encryption** – Some old satellites still transmit unencrypted data (yes, really).

☐ **Protocol Vulnerabilities** – Older satellite protocols like DVB-S weren't designed with modern cybersecurity threats in mind.

To counter these threats, we need stronger protocols, better encryption, and smarter cybersecurity practices across the board.

2. Hardening Satellite Communication Protocols: The Best Defenses

A. End-to-End Encryption: No More "Open" Satellite Signals

Many satellite protocols don't encrypt data by default, making it easy for attackers to intercept and manipulate transmissions.

✓ **Solution**: Use AES-256 encryption and end-to-end encryption (E2EE) for all communications.

🔒 **Example**: Modern military satellites encrypt everything, from GPS signals to reconnaissance imagery, so even if intercepted, it's useless without the decryption key.

B. Authentication & Access Control: No More Free Passes

Many satellite systems lack strong authentication mechanisms, allowing attackers to impersonate legitimate users.

✓ **Solution**: Implement multi-factor authentication (MFA) and digital certificates to verify only authorized entities can access satellites.

🔒 **Example**: NASA uses cryptographic authentication to ensure only approved ground stations can send commands to space probes.

C. Secure Firmware & OTA Updates: Patching Without Breaking the Satellite

Unlike your smartphone, a satellite can't just download a quick security patch—if something goes wrong, it stays wrong.

✓ **Solution**: Implement tamper-proof firmware updates and test them rigorously before deployment.

🔒 **Example**: SpaceX's Starlink satellites receive secure over-the-air (OTA) updates, preventing hackers from injecting malicious firmware.

D. Jamming & Spoofing Detection: Catching Cyber Attacks in Real-Time

GPS, weather, and communication satellites are vulnerable to jamming (blocking signals) and spoofing (sending fake signals).

✅ **Solution**: Deploy AI-powered intrusion detection to identify unusual traffic patterns and respond to attacks instantly.
🔒 **Example**: The U.S. Air Force's GPS III satellites use anti-spoofing tech to detect and filter out fake GPS signals.

E. Secure Ground Stations: The Most Overlooked Weak Point

Ground stations are often less secure than the satellites themselves—a single breach can give attackers full control over orbital assets.

✅ **Solution**: Implement zero-trust security models, segment networks, and use air-gapped systems to prevent unauthorized access.
🔒 **Example**: The European Space Agency (ESA) uses hardened ground stations with advanced firewalls and intrusion prevention systems.

3. Future Technologies for Next-Level Satellite Security

The battle against satellite hackers is ongoing, but emerging technologies could make it nearly impossible to compromise space-based systems.

🔏 **Quantum Encryption**: Using quantum key distribution (QKD), which is theoretically unhackable, to secure satellite transmissions.
🔏 **AI-Powered Threat Detection**: Using machine learning algorithms to identify cyberattacks in real-time.
🔏 **Blockchain for Satellite Security**: Using blockchain-based authentication to prevent unauthorized access and ensure data integrity.

Final Thoughts: Secure It or Lose It

If we don't lock down our satellites, we risk global communication blackouts, GPS failures, and even cyberwarfare in space. Whether it's encrypting signals, patching firmware, or deploying quantum-proof encryption, the future of satellite security depends on how well we protect our orbital assets today.

So, the next time you stream a movie via satellite internet, just remember—there's an army of cybersecurity experts working behind the scenes to make sure hackers aren't hijacking the connection and replacing your Netflix stream with… I don't know, an endless loop of Shrek 2 in Russian? 🚀😂

Chapter 3: Reconnaissance and Satellite Discovery Techniques

If you've ever tried to track down a rogue Bluetooth device in your house, you know the thrill of signal hunting. Now imagine doing the same thing—but for satellites. That's right, with the right tools and techniques, you can locate, track, and even analyze satellite signals without ever leaving your backyard. (Warning: Excessive interest in this topic may lead to an expensive SDR addiction and an uncontrollable urge to scan the skies.)

This chapter covers the reconnaissance phase of satellite security research, including identifying satellite signals using software-defined radios (SDRs), mapping satellite orbits using publicly available TLE data, and leveraging tools like Shodan and Censys to uncover exposed satellite infrastructure. We'll also explore passive and active signal analysis techniques, along with countermeasures designed to prevent unauthorized detection.

3.1 Identifying Satellite Signals Using SDR and Ground-Based Receivers

Tuning Into Space: Because Who Needs AM/FM When You Have Satellites?

Remember when you were a kid and you accidentally picked up your neighbor's baby monitor on your radio? Now imagine doing that… but with a satellite orbiting Earth. That's right—you can tune into space signals with the right tools, no astronaut license required.

Satellite signals are beaming all around us, carrying everything from TV broadcasts and GPS coordinates to military communications and even live feeds from the International Space Station. But how do you actually find and decode these signals without a billion-dollar ground station? The answer: Software-Defined Radio (SDR) and ground-based receivers.

Today, we're diving into the art and science of satellite signal hunting—whether you want to track weather satellites, eavesdrop on open signals, or just geek out with space tech. Let's grab our SDRs, point some antennas skyward, and see what's floating around in the ether.

1. Understanding How Satellite Signals Work

Before you start scanning the skies, you need to understand the basics of satellite communications.

☐ **Frequency Bands** – Satellites operate in specific radio frequency bands like L-band, S-band, C-band, and Ku-band.

☐ **Polarization** – Signals can be linear or circularly polarized, meaning you need the right type of antenna.

☐ **Modulation** – Satellites use AM/FM, QPSK, BPSK, and other digital modulations to transmit data.

☐ **Signal Strength** – Satellite signals are weak, so a good antenna and signal processing software are essential.

Now that we know what we're looking for, let's gear up.

2. Tools You Need for Satellite Signal Hunting

The best part about this? You don't need NASA's budget to get started—just some affordable SDR equipment and a bit of patience.

A. Software-Defined Radio (SDR) – Your Digital Ears

An SDR is like a radio scanner on steroids—it lets you tune into a wide range of frequencies, from air traffic control to deep space probes.

✅ **Beginner Option**: RTL-SDR (Cheap, ~$30, great for weather satellites)

✅ **Advanced Option**: HackRF One (Mid-range, ~$300, covers wider bands)

✅ **Expert Option**: LimeSDR or USRP (Pro-grade, ~$1,000+, used for deep-space and military signals)

B. Antennas – Your Satellite Signal Catchers

Not all antennas are created equal—picking the right one is crucial for tuning into specific satellites.

📡 **Discone Antennas** – Great for broadband signals (e.g., NOAA weather satellites).

📡 **Yagi Antennas** – Directional antennas for tracking moving satellites.

📡 **Helical Antennas** – Best for circularly polarized satellite signals.

C. Signal Processing Software – Turning Noise Into Data

Once you capture a signal, you need software to decode and analyze it.

🖵 **SDR# (SDRSharp)** – Good for beginners, basic signal visualization.
🖵 **GQRX** – Great for Linux and Mac users.
🖵 **GNURadio** – Advanced signal processing and decoding.
🖵 **Orbitron or GPredict** – Helps you track when and where satellites are passing over.

Now that we're geared up, let's catch some space signals!

3. Finding and Identifying Satellite Signals

So, where do you start scanning? Different satellites operate in different frequency bands. Here's a cheat sheet:

Satellite Type	Frequency Bands	Example Satellites
Weather Satellites	L-band (137 MHz)	NOAA, METEOR-M2
GPS Satellites	L1, L2 (1.5 GHz)	GPS, GLONASS, Galileo
TV Broadcast	C-band, Ku-band	DirecTV, Dish Network
Amateur Radio	UHF/VHF (145 MHz)	AO-91, AO-92 (Ham Sats)
Military/Spy Sats	X-band, Ka-band	Classified 🛰️

A. Step 1: Use Tracking Software to Find Satellites

Satellites don't stay still—they orbit Earth in predictable paths. Use Orbitron, GPredict, or Heavens-Above to check when a satellite is passing over your location.

B. Step 2: Tune Your SDR to the Right Frequency

Fire up SDR# or GQRX, and set your SDR to the known frequency of a satellite.

Adjust the bandwidth (usually 10 kHz to 1 MHz) to capture the full signal.

Watch for strong signals in the waterfall display—they appear as bright lines.

C. Step 3: Decode the Signal

For NOAA weather satellites, use WXtoImg to decode live weather maps.

For ham radio satellites, use multimode decoders like Fldigi to listen to voice transmissions.

For TV signals, you'll need a DVB-S demodulator (some free-to-air TV signals are unencrypted).

4. Fun Satellite Signals to Hunt For

Once you get the hang of it, satellite signal hunting can be addictive. Here are a few cool things to try:

🚀 **Listen to the ISS**: The International Space Station has an amateur radio station (145.800 MHz FM). Sometimes, astronauts even talk to ham radio operators on Earth!
☐ **Receive Live Weather Maps**: NOAA and METEOR-M2 satellites broadcast real-time weather imagery, which you can decode into actual cloud maps.
☐ **Decode GPS Signals**: GPS satellites send time signals that you can analyze—some researchers use them for precise scientific experiments.
📡 **Track Spy Satellites (Legally!)**: While their signals are encrypted, you can still track classified satellites using public orbital data.

5. Defensive Measures: How Satellites Prevent Unauthorized Signal Interception

Of course, not all signals are meant to be received by the public. Governments and corporations use several security measures to prevent eavesdropping:

🔒 **Encryption** – Military satellites use AES-256 encryption to prevent signal decoding.
🔒 **Frequency Hopping** – Some satellites change frequencies rapidly to evade detection.
🔒 **Directional Beaming** – Certain high-security satellites send signals only to designated receivers.

Still, many open signals are available for legal reception, making satellite scanning a fun and educational hobby (just don't do anything shady!).

Final Thoughts: The Universe Is Talking—Are You Listening?

Satellite signals are flying through the air around you right now—you just need the right tools to tune in and decode them. Whether you're tracking weather satellites, listening to astronaut radio chats, or mapping GPS signals, there's a whole world of space communications waiting to be explored.

So grab your SDR, point an antenna skyward, and start listening to space! Just don't blame me if you end up staying up all night tracking satellites like a true radio nerd. 🚀📡😄

3.2 Mapping and Tracking Satellites Using TLE Data and Orbital Mechanics

Spying on Space Junk: A Beginner's Guide to Satellite Stalking

Ever wonder how satellite TV companies, military agencies, and amateur radio nerds always know where a satellite is at any given time? No, they're not using crystal balls or space magic—they're using TLE data and orbital mechanics.

Tracking satellites is basically the space version of playing "Where's Waldo?"—except Waldo is a multimillion-dollar metal box zooming around Earth at 17,500 mph. And lucky for us, most satellite positions aren't a mystery! Thanks to Two-Line Element (TLE) sets, we can accurately predict where satellites will be at any time. Whether you want to track a spy satellite, a weather satellite, or just wave at the ISS as it flies over your backyard, this chapter will teach you how to map, track, and predict satellite movements like a pro.

1. What the Heck Is TLE Data?

TLE stands for Two-Line Element set, and it's essentially a math-packed text file that describes a satellite's orbit. NASA, NORAD, and amateur space enthusiasts use these numbers to predict satellite positions with shocking accuracy.

Example of a TLE Set (For the ISS)

ISS (ZARYA)

1 25544U 98067A   24093.54873843 .00002182 00000+0 50995-4 0 9994
2 25544 51.6457 77.6390 0007452 85.9998 274.1724 15.49146209433858

This may look like the Matrix wrote a love letter to NASA, but let's break it down:

Line 1: Identifies the satellite and metadata.

Line 2: Contains key orbital elements, such as:

Inclination (51.6°) – The tilt of the orbit relative to Earth's equator.

Eccentricity (0.0007) – How circular the orbit is.

RAAN, Arg of Perigee, Mean Anomaly – Fancy terms describing the orbit's orientation.

Mean Motion (15.49 rev/day) – How fast it orbits Earth.

Using these elements, we can precisely predict where the ISS (or any satellite) will be.

2. Tools to Track Satellites Using TLE Data

You don't need to manually crunch orbital calculations (unless you enjoy punishing your brain with math). Instead, use software that automatically interprets TLE data:

💻 **Orbitron** – Windows-based, real-time satellite tracking.
💻 **GPredict** – Open-source Linux/Mac/Windows software for amateur radio operators.
💻 **Heavens-Above** – Web-based tool for finding visible satellites.
💻 **NASA's HORIZONS System** – High-precision tracking for deep-space missions.

Simply input a TLE set, and these programs will map the satellite's path over Earth in real time.

3. How Orbital Mechanics Affects Satellite Motion

TLE data is only useful if you understand how satellites move. Orbital mechanics is essentially Newton's Laws in space—meaning objects stay in motion unless something (like Earth's atmosphere) slows them down.

Key Orbital Terms You Should Know

LEO (Low Earth Orbit) – Satellites at 200-2,000 km altitude, like the ISS and Starlink.

MEO (Medium Earth Orbit) – Satellites at 2,000-35,786 km, including GPS satellites.

GEO (Geostationary Orbit) – Satellites that hover over the same spot on Earth (like weather and TV satellites).

Inclination – The angle of the orbit relative to Earth's equator (e.g., polar orbits cover the whole planet).

Eccentricity – Measures how circular or elliptical the orbit is.

If you've ever thrown a rock, you've already experimented with orbital mechanics—except satellites are rocks that never stop falling, because they're moving so fast they "miss" the Earth.

4. Predicting Satellite Passes Over Your Location

Want to know when a satellite will fly overhead? Here's how to calculate future passes:

Step 1: Get the Latest TLE Data

Download TLE files from CelesTrak or Space-Track.org.

Copy and paste the TLE set for the satellite you want to track.

Step 2: Use Tracking Software

Open Orbitron or GPredict and input the TLE data.

Set your location (latitude/longitude).

The software will predict when the satellite will pass over your area.

Step 3: Look for Visible Passes (For Fun!)

Some satellites, like the ISS and Iridium satellites, reflect sunlight and are visible at night.

Use Heavens-Above to find when they'll be bright enough to see.

5. Tracking Classified and Military Satellites (Legally!)

Not all satellites are publicly listed. Governments don't want you tracking their spy satellites—but amateur astronomers have found ways to do it anyway.

☐ **Visual Tracking** – Using telescopes, enthusiasts manually log classified satellites.
⚑ **Radio Listening** – Even if TLE data is unavailable, some satellites still emit signals you can detect with SDR.
☐ **Community Data Sharing** – Websites like SatObs.org track secretive satellites based on amateur observations.

Some well-known "mystery satellites" include:

USA-245 – A classified reconnaissance satellite suspected of spying.

X-37B – A secretive, reusable space plane operated by the U.S. Air Force.

Yaogan Satellites – Chinese military surveillance satellites.

6. How Satellites Avoid Detection and Tracking

Governments don't like their satellites being tracked, so they've developed clever ways to stay hidden:

☐☐ **Orbital Maneuvers** – Military satellites sometimes change orbits unexpectedly.
☐☐ **Stealth Coatings** – Some satellites use radar-absorbing materials to be harder to track.
☐☐ **Low-Power Transmissions** – Spy satellites often emit weak signals to avoid detection.

But, despite these tricks, amateur trackers often find them anyway. So if you're into space espionage, welcome to the club.

Final Thoughts: Welcome to the World of Space Stalking

Tracking satellites is both an art and a science. Whether you're mapping Starlink constellations, predicting ISS flyovers, or playing space detective with secret spy sats, TLE data and orbital mechanics give you the power to follow anything that flies above Earth.

So next time you're outside staring at the night sky, just remember: one of those twinkling lights might actually be a billion-dollar satellite watching you back. 😆

3.3 Using Shodan and Censys to Find Exposed Satellite Systems

The Google for Hackers: Finding Satellites the Easy Way

Remember when you were a kid and you'd use Google to find answers to homework questions instead of actually reading the textbook? Well, Shodan and Censys are kind of like that—except instead of looking up math equations, you're finding vulnerable satellite systems exposed on the internet.

And trust me, they're out there.

Most people think satellites are ultra-secure, floating in space with laser shields and government firewalls. But in reality? Many satellite control systems, ground stations, and data relays are connected to the internet—sometimes with default passwords still intact. It's the equivalent of leaving your front door wide open in a bad neighborhood and hoping no one notices.

So in this chapter, we're diving into how to use Shodan and Censys to discover exposed satellite systems, how attackers leverage these tools, and how to protect against these risks.

1. What Are Shodan and Censys?

If Google indexes websites, Shodan and Censys index internet-connected devices—routers, webcams, industrial control systems, and, yes, even satellite infrastructure.

Shodan: The Search Engine for Everything Connected

Shodan scans the internet for open ports, services, and devices, creating a massive database of connected systems. With just a few queries, you can find:

Satellite ground station terminals

Exposed VSAT (Very Small Aperture Terminal) systems

Unsecured satellite telemetry dashboards

Open ports for remote management (Telnet, SSH, RDP)

Shodan's motto? "The world's most dangerous search engine." And they're not wrong.

Censys: A More Detailed Cyber Intel Tool

Censys works similarly to Shodan but dives deeper into SSL certificates, encryption methods, and device metadata. It's used by cybersecurity pros, researchers, and, of course, anyone curious about what's lurking on the internet.

Unlike Shodan, which is more about finding devices, Censys excels at analyzing security flaws and vulnerabilities in those devices.

2. Finding Satellite Systems with Shodan and Censys

So how do we actually find satellite-related systems using these tools? Here are some powerful Shodan search queries to get you started:

Finding Open Satellite Terminals

VSAT port:23,22

(Finds VSAT satellite terminals with Telnet or SSH access—often exposed with weak credentials.)

Locating Satellite Communication Equipment

"Intellian" OR "HughesNet" OR "iDirect" OR "Inmarsat"

(This query reveals popular satellite modems and ground station hardware.)

Exposed Satellite Dashboards

"http.title:Satellite" OR "http.title:Telemetry" OR "http.title:Ground Station"

(Finds web-based control panels for satellite telemetry and tracking.)

Censys Query for Open Satellite Services

services.service_name: "telnet" AND services.banner: "Welcome"

(Locates systems running Telnet with generic welcome banners, which often indicates weak security.)

3. Real-World Examples of Exposed Satellite Systems

Attackers have used Shodan and Censys to find and exploit real-world satellite vulnerabilities. Here are a few shocking examples:

🏧 **Exposed VSAT Terminals** – Security researchers discovered thousands of VSAT terminals online with no authentication, allowing attackers to hijack satellite internet connections.

🏧 **Unprotected Satellite Telemetry Panels** – In 2018, unsecured satellite control dashboards were found publicly accessible, meaning anyone could tamper with system settings.

🏧 **Hacked Maritime and Aviation Systems** – Cybercriminals have used default credentials on Shodan-discovered satellite communication systems to disrupt ships and airplanes.

And if researchers are finding these vulnerabilities, you can bet nation-state hackers and cybercriminals are too.

4. How Attackers Exploit These Exposed Systems

Once an attacker finds a satellite-related system, the next steps typically follow this pattern:

1️ Check for Default Credentials – Many devices use default logins like:

admin:admin

root:password

operator:1234

Attackers try these first—and, shockingly, they still work far too often.

2☐ Scan for Vulnerabilities – If the system requires authentication, attackers use tools like Metasploit or Nmap to look for known security flaws.

3☐ Exploit Weak Encryption – Older satellite communication protocols often use weak or outdated encryption, making them susceptible to brute force attacks.

4☐ MITM Attacks on Data Traffic – Attackers can intercept and manipulate satellite internet traffic, allowing them to spy on communications or even inject malicious data.

5. Defending Against Shodan and Censys Exposure

If you're running a satellite-based system, or just want to avoid getting caught with your digital pants down, here's how to protect against these risks:

✅ **Remove Unnecessary Internet Exposure** – If a system doesn't need to be online, don't put it online.

✅ **Use Strong Authentication** – Default passwords are an open invitation to hackers. Use strong, unique passwords and enable multi-factor authentication (MFA) where possible.

✅ **Encrypt Communications** – Ensure all satellite uplinks, telemetry data, and ground station connections use strong encryption methods like AES-256 or TLS 1.3.

✅ **Firewall and Access Controls** – Restrict access to trusted IPs only and block unnecessary ports and services.

✅ **Regular Security Audits** – Run periodic Shodan and Censys scans on your own infrastructure to see what's exposed—before attackers do.

Final Thoughts: Shodan and Censys—Friend or Foe?

Shodan and Censys are just tools—like a hammer, they can be used for construction or destruction. Security researchers and ethical hackers use them to identify and fix vulnerabilities, while malicious actors use them to find easy targets.

At the end of the day, if you're managing satellite communications or IoT devices, the key takeaway is this:

🚀 If it's on Shodan, it's vulnerable. If it's on Censys, it's even worse.

So before your satellite internet system, ground station, or space IoT device becomes the next big cyber attack headline—lock it down.

3.4 Passive and Active Signal Analysis in Space IoT Networks

Spying on Satellites: The Art of Listening (and Talking) to Space

Ever wanted to eavesdrop on satellites like some kind of space-age spy? Well, you're in luck! Because in the world of Space IoT networks, signals are flying around unprotected more often than you'd think. Whether it's weather satellites, maritime communications, or even GPS signals, there's a lot happening up there, and not all of it is properly secured.

Now, before you get too excited, let me just say: Don't go trying to hijack a satellite unless you enjoy government agents knocking on your door at 3 AM. This chapter is all about understanding how satellite signals are analyzed—both passively (listening) and actively (interacting or interfering)—so you can learn how to defend against these vulnerabilities rather than exploit them.

Sound cool? Good. Let's dive in.

1. What is Passive and Active Signal Analysis?

Passive Signal Analysis = Just listening. Like a radio tuner picking up FM stations, passive analysis involves capturing and decoding satellite signals without interacting with the system itself.

Active Signal Analysis = Talking back. This involves sending signals to the satellite or ground station, modifying transmissions, or even attempting to interfere with operations. This is where things get legally and ethically dicey.

Let's break them both down.

2. Passive Signal Analysis: Listening to Space Without Getting Caught

Passive analysis is completely legal (mostly). You're just receiving signals that satellites are already broadcasting, much like how anyone with a radio can pick up AM/FM stations. Here's how it works:

Tools for Passive Signal Analysis

To analyze satellite signals, you'll need some basic software-defined radio (SDR) hardware:

✅ **RTL-SDR** – A cheap USB receiver that can pick up a variety of signals.
✅ **HackRF One** – A more advanced SDR with wider frequency range.
✅ **USRP (Universal Software Radio Peripheral)** – The big leagues of SDRs, used by researchers and professionals.

Pair these with some signal analysis software, and you're in business:

◆ **GQRX or SDR# (SDR Sharp)** – Basic tools for visualizing and tuning into signals.
◆ **GNURadio** – Open-source software for advanced signal processing.
◆ **SatDump** – Specifically designed for decoding satellite signals.

What Can You Listen to?

Weather Satellites (NOAA, METEOR, GOES) – They broadcast unencrypted images of cloud patterns and weather data.

Maritime and Aviation Communications (Inmarsat, Iridium) – Ships and planes use satellite systems to send position reports.

Amateur Radio Satellites (AMSAT, CubeSats) – Ham radio operators use satellites for global communication.

GNSS Signals (GPS, Galileo, GLONASS, BeiDou) – While encrypted for military use, civilian navigation signals are openly available.

All of these signals can be captured and analyzed, sometimes even decoded into meaningful data—without ever transmitting anything back.

3. Active Signal Analysis: Talking to Satellites (or Messing with Them)

Now things get a little more... sketchy.

Active signal analysis means you're transmitting signals, modifying communications, or interacting with a satellite in some way. This could be for ethical research (like testing security flaws) or malicious activities (like jamming signals or hijacking communications).

Types of Active Signal Analysis

🛰️ **Replay Attacks** – Capturing a satellite's transmission and then rebroadcasting it to trick the system into accepting fake data.

🛰️ **MITM (Man-in-the-Middle) Attacks** – Intercepting and modifying real-time satellite communications, often used for espionage.

🛰️ **GPS Spoofing** – Sending fake GPS signals to mislead navigation systems. (This has been used in military cyberwarfare.)

🛰️ **Uplink Injection** – Attempting to send commands to a satellite (illegal unless you own the satellite).

🛰️ **Denial of Service (Jamming)** – Blocking legitimate signals by overwhelming the frequency with noise.

4. Real-World Examples of Satellite Signal Exploits

📷 **GPS Spoofing in Iran (2011)**

The Iranian military allegedly hijacked a U.S. military drone by spoofing GPS signals, tricking it into landing in Iran instead of returning to base.

📷 **Russian GPS Spoofing Attacks**

Russian cyber units have repeatedly been caught jamming and spoofing GPS signals, particularly around military installations and VIP movements.

📷 **Unauthorized Satellite TV Hijacking**

In 1986, a hacker known as "Captain Midnight" took over HBO's satellite feed, broadcasting a protest message instead.

These cases highlight how vulnerable space-based systems can be—especially if proper encryption and authentication aren't in place.

5. Protecting Against Passive and Active Signal Threats

If you're responsible for securing satellite communications, here's how to protect against passive and active attacks:

✅ **Use Strong Encryption** – Any sensitive satellite transmission should be end-to-end encrypted with modern cryptographic protocols (AES-256, PQC).

✅ **Authenticate Commands** – Satellites should verify who's sending commands before accepting them (e.g., digital signatures).

✅ **Frequency Hopping** – A technique where signals rapidly switch frequencies, making interception and jamming more difficult.

✅ **Directional Beamforming** – Satellites should focus signals only where they need to go, reducing unintended interception.

✅ **Anti-Jamming Technologies** – Techniques like adaptive filtering can help satellites ignore interference from attackers.

Final Thoughts: The Fine Line Between Research and Cybercrime

Passive signal analysis? Totally fine. It's like listening to a podcast—you're just receiving what's already out there.

Active signal analysis? That's where things get dicey. The moment you start transmitting, you're playing in a legal gray area that can quickly turn into a felony.

So, if you're experimenting with space IoT security, keep it ethical. Because while understanding vulnerabilities is important, becoming a wanted cybercriminal is probably not a career goal (unless you want to be the next "Captain Midnight"). 🚀

3.5 Countermeasures to Prevent Unauthorized Satellite Detection

Keeping Your Satellite Off the Grid (Good Luck Hiding in Space!)

Ah, the joys of being a satellite in low Earth orbit—you're shining brightly, beaming signals across the planet, and broadcasting your location like a giant cosmic billboard. If satellites had egos, they'd be the ultimate social media influencers.

But here's the problem: not everyone should know where your satellite is or what it's transmitting. Hackers, spies, and even overenthusiastic researchers armed with software-defined radios (SDRs) and open-source tracking tools love to sniff out exposed satellites. And if they can see you, they can target you.

So, how do you make a satellite less visible, less vulnerable, and less of a hacker's dream project? Buckle up, because we're about to dive into the world of stealth satellites, signal obfuscation, and next-level security tricks to keep unauthorized eyes (and ears) away.

1. Why Do People Want to Detect Satellites in the First Place?

Before we get into how to hide, let's answer why someone might want to find a satellite in the first place. There are three main reasons:

🔍 **Reconnaissance & Espionage** – Governments and cybercriminals want to track satellite positions and frequencies to intercept or manipulate communications.

🔍 **Signal Hijacking & Eavesdropping** – If an attacker knows your satellite's frequency, they can passively listen in or even attempt a MITM (Man-in-the-Middle) attack.

🔍 **Jamming & Disruption** – Bad actors can locate satellite signals and jam them, effectively denying service to legitimate users.

The good news? There are countermeasures to make sure your satellite isn't an open invitation for attackers.

2. Techniques to Prevent Satellite Detection

☐☐ A. Using Low-Probability-of-Intercept (LPI) Signals

If you don't want someone finding your satellite signal, the best approach is not making it obvious in the first place. This is where Low-Probability-of-Intercept (LPI) communications come in.

- **Frequency Hopping Spread Spectrum (FHSS):** Constantly changes frequencies, making it hard for adversaries to lock onto your signal.
- **Direct Sequence Spread Spectrum (DSSS):** Spreads the signal over a wider band, making it harder to distinguish from background noise.
- **Burst Transmissions**: Instead of a continuous stream, data is sent in short, powerful bursts, reducing the time an attacker has to intercept it.

Think of it like whispering secrets in a crowded room versus shouting them over a megaphone—it's all about reducing visibility.

B. Directional Antennas & Beamforming

- Most satellite signals are broadcast openly, meaning anyone with an SDR and a decent antenna can pick them up.

- **Solution**? Use highly directional antennas to focus transmissions only where they need to go. The narrower the beam, the harder it is for an eavesdropper to intercept signals.

- **Adaptive Beamforming**: Uses AI to constantly adjust signal direction, avoiding interception from known hostile areas.

If a satellite doesn't need to talk to the whole planet, why broadcast like it does?

C. Encrypt EVERYTHING (No, Seriously, EVERYTHING)

If someone does manage to detect your satellite signal, the next best defense is strong encryption. This seems obvious, but you'd be shocked how many satellites still transmit unencrypted data (looking at you, older weather and maritime systems).

✓ **End-to-End Encryption (E2EE)** – Ensure that data is encrypted before it's sent and only decrypted at the receiving end.
✓ **Quantum Cryptography** – Some next-gen satellites are starting to use quantum key distribution (QKD) for unbreakable encryption.
✓ **Self-Destructing Keys** – Some military satellites regularly destroy and regenerate encryption keys, preventing long-term interception.

The lesson here? Even if someone finds your signal, make sure they can't read a damn thing.

3. Defending Against Open-Source Satellite Tracking

One of the biggest challenges in preventing unauthorized satellite detection is that satellite tracking isn't just for spies anymore. Enthusiasts, amateur astronomers, and hackers use publicly available data to track and predict satellite orbits.

Here's how to make it harder for the average person to find your satellite:

▢▢ A. Randomized Orbital Maneuvers

🚀 Most satellites follow predictable orbits, making them easy to track.
🚀 Solution? Periodically alter the orbit slightly, throwing off public databases.
🚀 Military and intelligence satellites already use this trick to reduce tracking accuracy.

📡 B. Avoiding Publicly Available TLE Data

🚀 Two-Line Element Sets (TLEs) are orbital parameters published by organizations like NORAD and CelesTrak.
🚀 If you want to keep your satellite off the radar, limit how much of this data is publicly shared.

🔍 C. Using Optical Stealth Techniques

🚀 Some satellites use low-reflectivity coatings or position themselves to minimize sunlight reflection, making them harder to track visually.
🚀 There are even proposals for electronic cloaking to mask thermal and radio signatures.

Basically, the more unpredictable and hard-to-see your satellite is, the better.

4. Anti-Jamming and Signal Integrity Protection

Even if your satellite is well-hidden, attackers can still try to jam its signals. Here's how to fight back:

✓ **Adaptive Power Control** – Increases signal strength only when necessary, reducing exposure to potential jammers.

✓ **Anti-Jamming Modulation** – Advanced waveforms like orthogonal frequency-division multiplexing (OFDM) help reduce jamming effects.

✓ **AI-Powered Intrusion Detection** – Machine learning algorithms can detect and block unauthorized signal manipulation.

If you can't hide, at least make yourself extremely annoying to attack.

Final Thoughts: You Can't Hide Forever, But You Can Make It Hard as Hell

Let's be honest—hiding a satellite completely is nearly impossible. Space is big, but signals spread out fast, and with modern tracking tools, determined hackers and nation-states can eventually find what they're looking for.

But here's the key takeaway:

The harder you make it to detect and intercept your satellite's signals, the fewer attackers will bother trying.

So, while you won't make your satellite completely invisible, you can definitely throw enough obstacles in the way to make life very, very annoying for cybercriminals.

And in cybersecurity, being a pain in the ass to hack is often the best defense. 🚀

Chapter 4: Attacking Satellite Communication Links

You ever wish you could just "borrow" premium satellite TV without paying? Well, that's illegal—don't do that. But if you've ever been curious about how signals can be intercepted, manipulated, or even hijacked, you're in for a treat. Satellite communication links are often way less secure than you'd expect, making them prime targets for attackers looking to eavesdrop or even launch full-blown Man-in-the-Middle (MITM) attacks.

This chapter dives into the mechanics of uplink and downlink communications, explaining how attackers intercept satellite data, break weak encryption, and manipulate transmissions. We'll cover real-world cases of signal hijacking and analyze methods to secure satellite links against unauthorized access, ensuring the integrity and confidentiality of space-based communication.

4.1 Understanding Uplink and Downlink Communications

Why Satellites Are Like Overly Complicated Walkie-Talkies

Ever had a really bad phone call where one person keeps talking over the other because of a delay? That's basically satellite communications—except instead of annoying your friend, you're potentially delaying critical data transmissions across the planet.

Satellites communicate in two fundamental ways: uplink (sending signals to space) and downlink (receiving signals back on Earth). Think of it like a celestial game of catch—but instead of a ball, we're tossing packets of data across thousands of miles using radio waves.

And just like a walkie-talkie, if someone intercepts, jams, or manipulates the signal, things can go horribly wrong. Imagine watching a live stream from the International Space Station, only to have someone replace the astronaut's broadcast with cat videos—or worse, malicious commands that could alter satellite operations.

If you've ever wondered how global internet, GPS, and military-grade surveillance works—or how hackers mess with it—you're in for a ride. Welcome to the crazy world of uplink and downlink hacking.

What Is Uplink and Downlink?

To put it simply:

Uplink → Earth to Space 🚀 (Commands, data uploads, control signals)

Downlink → Space to Earth □ (Telemetry, images, broadcasts, navigation signals)

Each satellite relies on ground stations to send and receive these signals, using specific radio frequencies to avoid interference.

But here's where things get interesting (and dangerous): If an attacker gains control of uplink signals, they can send unauthorized commands. If they mess with downlink signals, they can intercept, jam, or spoof data.

Let's break it down.

The Uplink: Talking to Satellites (Earth → Space)

The uplink is the command center of satellite operations. Every time NASA, SpaceX, or a telecom company sends a command to a satellite, it's an uplink transmission.

□□ **What Gets Sent on Uplink?**

Software updates & firmware patches

Control commands (changing orbit, adjusting antennas, modifying signal frequencies)

Encryption keys & authentication data

Sensor configurations & data requests

🚀 **Security Risks in Uplink Communications**

Unauthorized Command Injection – A hacker could impersonate a ground station and send rogue commands.

Signal Jamming – Attackers can block uplink signals, preventing the satellite from receiving crucial updates.

Replay Attacks – If a hacker captures and replays a previously authenticated command, they can fool the satellite into executing it again.

Imagine if someone took control of a GPS satellite and slightly shifted its coordinates—that's the difference between your Uber driver finding you or ending up in another city.

The Downlink: Receiving Data from Space (Space → Earth)

The downlink is where satellites send back all the data they collect. This includes:

📡 What Gets Transmitted on Downlink?

Satellite images & surveillance footage

GPS navigation signals

Internet data (like Starlink and satellite ISPs)

Weather and climate data

Scientific telemetry (radiation levels, atmospheric data)

🎯 Security Risks in Downlink Communications

Eavesdropping & Data Interception – Hackers with an SDR (software-defined radio) can listen in on unencrypted satellite data.

Man-in-the-Middle Attacks – Attackers can intercept and modify downlink data before it reaches the ground station.

Signal Spoofing – Someone could broadcast fake GPS signals, misleading entire fleets of ships, planes, or even military assets.

If you've ever wondered how hackers pull off GPS spoofing attacks to confuse drones or ships, this is it.

Frequencies Used in Uplink & Downlink

Satellites don't use just one frequency—they operate across multiple bands to handle different types of communications.

Frequency Band	Uplink Range	Downlink Range	Usage Example
L-band	1.6 GHz	1.5 GHz	GPS, maritime satellites
S-band	2.0 - 2.3 GHz	2.2 - 2.3 GHz	Telemetry, space research
C-band	5.9 - 6.4 GHz	3.7 - 4.2 GHz	Satellite TV, weather satellites
X-band	7.9 - 8.4 GHz	7.2 - 7.8 GHz	Military and deep space comms
Ku-band	14.0 - 14.5 GHz	10.7 - 12.75 GHz	Satellite internet (Starlink, HughesNet)
Ka-band	27.5 - 31.0 GHz	17.7 - 21.2 GHz	High-speed broadband, military

Higher frequency bands like Ku and Ka provide faster data rates, but they are more susceptible to interference (like rain fade).

That's why hackers and security researchers focus on low-band signals (L & S) since they travel further and are used in critical services like GPS.

Defending Against Uplink & Downlink Attacks

So, how do we protect satellites from hackers and bad actors? Here are some countermeasures:

✅ **Strong Encryption** – All commands sent to a satellite should be end-to-end encrypted to prevent interception and spoofing.

✅ **Authentication & Access Control** – Only authorized ground stations should be able to send commands, using multi-factor authentication.

✅ **Frequency Hopping** – Rapidly switching frequencies makes it harder for attackers to jam or intercept transmissions.

✅ **Directional Antennas** – Beamforming reduces the chance of signals being intercepted by unauthorized receivers.

✅ **Anomaly Detection AI** – Machine learning can detect unusual commands and prevent unauthorized control.

If a hacker tries sending rogue commands, an AI-based system could flag it as suspicious and ignore it before any damage is done.

Final Thoughts: Hackers Love Space, But You Can Make Their Life Miserable

Here's the truth: satellites weren't built with cybersecurity in mind. Many still use outdated encryption, and some still transmit unprotected data (yes, even in 2025!).

If you're serious about securing space communications, the best approach is locking down uplink access and encrypting downlink transmissions. The harder you make it for hackers to manipulate signals, the safer global communications will be.

And remember—if your satellite gets hacked, you're not just losing data. You might wake up to find your satellite rerouted to play Rick Astley's "Never Gonna Give You Up" on a government channel. Don't let that be your legacy. 🚀

4.2 Signal Interception and Eavesdropping on Satellite Data

Spying on Satellites: Like Wiretapping, but in Space

If you ever wanted to feel like a secret agent without the risk of getting arrested, eavesdropping on satellite signals is the closest you'll get. Unlike terrestrial networks, where data is often encrypted and hidden behind layers of security, many satellite communications are still transmitted in the open, ripe for interception by anyone with the right tools.

Think about it—satellites beam signals down to Earth, covering massive areas. If you can tune in to the right frequency, you're essentially listening to a giant cosmic radio station broadcasting sensitive information. Want to hear live maritime communications? No problem. Looking for weather satellite feeds? Easy. Tracking military logistics? Well... that's a bit more illegal, but technically still possible.

Signal interception is a major cybersecurity threat because it doesn't even require hacking into a satellite—you just passively collect the data as it flies through space. No need to break in. No need to send rogue commands. Just sit back, tune in, and enjoy the show.

How Satellite Signal Interception Works

Satellite transmissions work by broadcasting data from space to Earth using radio frequencies. Since these signals are often omnidirectional or wide-beam, they spread over vast areas, making them relatively easy to pick up if you have the right equipment.

🔍 How Attackers Intercept Satellite Signals:

Use a Software-Defined Radio (SDR): Devices like HackRF, BladeRF, or Ettus USRP can tune into satellite frequencies.

Find the Right Frequency: Public and private databases list the frequencies used by different satellites.

Capture the Signal: Using SDR software like GQRX, SDR#, or GNU Radio, attackers can record raw satellite data.

Demodulate & Decode: Many signals are unencrypted or use weak encoding, making them easy to convert into readable data.

Analyze and Exploit: From intercepted phone calls to sensitive corporate data, the possibilities are endless (and dangerous).

Some military and government satellites use narrow-beam transmissions and encryption, making interception harder—but commercial, scientific, and even some weather satellites still transmit openly.

Types of Satellite Signals That Can Be Intercepted

Satellite eavesdropping isn't just theoretical—it's been happening for decades. Here are some real-world examples of signals that can be intercepted:

🛰 Satellite Internet Traffic

Many satellite ISPs still transmit data in cleartext (HTTP, FTP, VoIP).

Hackers have intercepted emails, passwords, and even live video calls from unencrypted satellite links.

☐ Weather and Remote Sensing Data

Satellites send raw weather images, climate data, and environmental readings without encryption.

Researchers and hackers can capture live satellite imagery using SDRs.

⚓ Maritime & Aviation Communications

Ships and aircraft use satellite-based tracking systems (AIS & ACARS) that broadcast location data openly.

Hackers have intercepted live cockpit communications and even faked ship positions using spoofing techniques.

🛰 Military & Government Transmissions (High Risk!)

Some older military satellites still use outdated encryption, making them potential targets.

There have been cases of spy agencies intercepting enemy satellite traffic for intelligence gathering.

If you think this all sounds like a bad spy movie, think again—these attacks happen in real life, and satellite operators are racing to fix these vulnerabilities.

Real-World Incidents of Satellite Interception

Hackers and intelligence agencies have been snooping on satellite transmissions for decades. Here are a few notable cases:

🛰 Project Echelon (NSA & Allies)

A secret surveillance program that monitored global satellite communications.

Used to intercept military, political, and commercial transmissions worldwide.

📡 Satellite Internet Hack (2009-2014)

European researchers intercepted internet traffic from commercial satellite ISPs.

Captured emails, passwords, and sensitive corporate data without needing direct access.

🛰 ACARS Aviation Eavesdropping

Hackers intercepted live aircraft communications via satellite.

Exposed flight paths, crew messages, and even passenger reservation details.

🚢 AIS Ship Tracking Manipulation

Researchers intercepted live ship GPS data and spoofed vessel locations.

Showed ships sailing in the middle of deserts or disappearing completely.

These incidents prove that satellite eavesdropping is not science fiction—it's a real cybersecurity threat that governments and industries need to address immediately.

How to Protect Against Satellite Eavesdropping

So, if hackers can just listen in on satellite transmissions, how do we stop them? Here are some critical defense strategies:

✓ Encryption, Encryption, Encryption!

End-to-end encryption (AES-256, Quantum Encryption) should be mandatory for all satellite transmissions.

Many older satellites still use weak or no encryption—this needs to change.

✓ Frequency Hopping & Spread Spectrum Techniques

Constantly changing frequencies makes it harder for attackers to lock onto signals.

Used in military and high-security satellite communications.

✓ Directional Antennas & Beamforming

Using focused, narrow-beam antennas reduces signal exposure to eavesdroppers.

Many modern satellites are adopting highly directional transmission methods.

✓ AI-Based Anomaly Detection

Machine learning can detect unusual interception attempts and alert security teams.

AI-powered satellite security is becoming a key defense strategy.

✅ Regulatory Policies & Industry Standards

Governments and agencies like FCC, ITU, and ESA are pushing for stronger encryption standards.

The push for quantum encryption in space is gaining traction to prevent future eavesdropping.

Final Thoughts: Don't Let Hackers Tune In on Your Space Secrets

Let's be real—space should be awesome, not insecure. But as it turns out, satellite signals are one of the easiest things to hack, and eavesdroppers have been exploiting this for decades.

The good news? The industry is finally waking up to the dangers of unencrypted transmissions, and new security measures are being deployed. But until every satellite follows modern encryption standards, hackers will keep tuning in—and your private data might just end up broadcasted across the cosmos.

If you're in charge of a satellite network, encrypt your signals. If you're a hacker... well, maybe find a legal job in cybersecurity instead of accidentally messing with military satellites. 🚀

4.3 Man-in-the-Middle (MITM) Attacks on Satellite Transmissions

MITM in Space: Because Hacking Satellites is More Fun Than Wi-Fi

Let's be honest—most people hear "Man-in-the-Middle attack" and think about some coffee shop hacker stealing passwords over free Wi-Fi. But why settle for hacking a random dude's Instagram when you can go bigger—like intercepting and manipulating satellite transmissions?

That's right. MITM attacks aren't just for hackers lurking on public networks—they work in space, too. The difference? Instead of snooping on someone's online shopping, you're messing with signals that control drones, ships, planes, and entire global communication networks. No big deal, right?

MITM attacks on satellite systems allow attackers to intercept, alter, or completely manipulate data flowing between satellites and ground stations. Want to reroute GPS signals? Tamper with financial transactions? Spoof military communications? If done right, an MITM attack in space can disrupt entire industries or even geopolitical stability.

Scary? Absolutely. Possible? 100%. Preventable? Only if we get serious about satellite security.

How MITM Attacks Work in Satellite Communications

A MITM attack happens when an attacker secretly positions themselves between two communicating parties—in this case, a satellite and a ground station. Unlike eavesdropping, where attackers just listen in, MITM attackers actively manipulate the data before it reaches its destination.

🔍 How Hackers Perform MITM Attacks on Satellite Links:

1️⃣ Intercepting Satellite Signals

Attackers use Software-Defined Radios (SDRs) and large antennas to capture downlink signals.

With the right frequency and modulation knowledge, they can decode and analyze the data.

2️⃣ Impersonating a Legitimate Communication Party

The attacker spoofs the satellite or the ground station by relaying modified data.

If authentication is weak, the system won't even realize it's been hijacked.

3️⃣ Altering or Injecting Malicious Data

Attackers can modify navigation signals, leading to GPS spoofing attacks.

Sensitive data like financial transactions or military communications can be altered or blocked.

4⃞ Relaying Fake or Delayed Information

Attackers introduce timing delays to disrupt operations (e.g., delaying stock market trades that rely on satellite timestamps).

In military scenarios, fake intelligence reports can be sent to mislead operations.

The key to a successful MITM attack? The victim must not realize that anything is wrong—until it's too late.

Real-World MITM Attacks on Satellites

🚀 GPS Spoofing Attacks (Iran, 2011)

Iranian forces allegedly spoofed GPS signals to hijack a U.S. RQ-170 Sentinel drone.

By intercepting and modifying navigation signals, they tricked the drone into landing in Iran instead of its original base.

💰 Financial Market Attacks via Satellite (2019)

Researchers demonstrated how MITM attacks on satellite-based financial systems could be used to delay or alter stock market trades.

Some high-frequency trading firms rely on satellite timestamps, making them vulnerable to timing manipulation.

⚓ Maritime GPS Spoofing (Black Sea, 2017)

Ships in the Black Sea reported GPS anomalies, with their locations appearing miles inland.

Analysts suspect it was a MITM attack or GPS spoofing experiment by a nation-state actor.

These examples prove that MITM attacks on satellite transmissions aren't just theoretical—they're already happening.

The Dangers of MITM Attacks on Satellites

A successful MITM attack on a satellite system can lead to serious real-world consequences:

⬜⬜ Military and Intelligence Disruptions

Attackers can alter satellite communications between military forces, causing misinformation in combat scenarios.

Spies could intercept and modify classified transmissions, leading to compromised operations.

📡 Telecommunications Hijacking

Satellite-based phone calls, TV broadcasts, and internet services can be intercepted and manipulated.

Attackers could spread disinformation or inject propaganda into media channels.

🚢 Navigation and Transportation Disruptions

Fake GPS signals could mislead planes, ships, and autonomous vehicles.

Attackers could reroute supply chains or cause traffic chaos.

🏛 Financial Market Manipulation

Stock markets relying on satellite timestamps could be exploited for fraudulent trading.

Time-sensitive financial transactions could be delayed or modified.

⬜⬜ Space-Based Cyberwarfare

Nation-state hackers could intercept enemy satellite communications to sabotage space missions.

Attackers could alter satellite control commands, potentially leading to collisions or system failures.

MITM attacks on satellites don't just affect cybersecurity—they can destabilize entire industries and national security.

How to Defend Against Satellite MITM Attacks

So, how do we stop attackers from inserting themselves into satellite communications? Here are the most critical defenses:

✅ **Strong Encryption & Authentication**

All satellite communications should use end-to-end encryption (AES-256, PQC, or quantum cryptography).

Mutual authentication must be enforced between satellites and ground stations.

✅ **Frequency Hopping & Spread Spectrum**

Dynamic frequency changes make it harder for attackers to intercept and relay signals.

This technique is already used in military and high-security satellite systems.

✅ **Tamper-Proof Signal Integrity Verification**

Advanced cryptographic techniques can verify that satellite data hasn't been altered in transit.

Digital signatures and watermarking can detect unauthorized modifications.

✅ **AI-Based Anomaly Detection**

Machine learning can monitor satellite traffic patterns and detect suspicious relay behavior.

AI-driven security platforms can automatically flag potential MITM attacks.

✅ **Regulatory Compliance & Cybersecurity Standards**

Governments and agencies like FCC, ITU, and ESA must enforce stricter security protocols for satellite operators.

Future satellite networks should integrate zero-trust security architectures.

Final Thoughts: Secure Your Signals or Get Hacked from Space

MITM attacks on satellite transmissions are like Wi-Fi hacking on steroids—except instead of stealing someone's Netflix password, you're manipulating global navigation systems, financial transactions, and military operations.

The scary part? Many satellites still lack proper encryption and authentication, making these attacks way too easy for skilled hackers.

The good news? With strong encryption, AI-driven anomaly detection, and better regulatory policies, we can make satellite MITM attacks significantly harder to pull off.

So, if you're working on satellite security, take this seriously—because the next hacker looking to exploit your satellite might just be sitting in a garage with a laptop, an SDR, and a dream. 🚀

4.4 Brute-Forcing and Cracking Weak Encryption in Satellite Networks

Breaking Satellite Encryption: Because Space Needs Better Passwords Than "123456" Look, if you've ever brute-forced your way into a forgotten Wi-Fi router, you already know the thrill of cracking weak encryption. Now, imagine doing the same thing—but with satellites.

That's right. Some satellite systems, especially older ones, are about as secure as an email account from 1999. Weak passwords, outdated encryption schemes, and lazy security implementations mean some satellite communications are just begging to be cracked.

And when bad actors break satellite encryption? They're not just stealing grandma's Netflix login. They're intercepting classified military data, manipulating GPS signals, hijacking satellite-controlled drones, or even messing with global financial transactions. Sounds like a sci-fi movie, right? Well, welcome to reality.

But how does this actually work? Let's dive into the dark arts of brute-forcing and cracking weak encryption in satellite networks—and, more importantly, how we can stop it.

Understanding Satellite Encryption (Or the Lack of It)

Encryption is supposed to keep satellite communications secure by scrambling the data so that only authorized parties can read it. But here's the problem:

● Weak or Outdated Encryption Algorithms

Some older satellites still use DES (Data Encryption Standard), which was broken decades ago.

Even some modern satellites use weak or improperly implemented AES encryption.

● Default and Hardcoded Keys

Some satellites have hardcoded encryption keys in their firmware.

Others use default keys that can be found in public manuals or research papers.

● Lazy or No Authentication

Some satellites don't even bother encrypting their transmissions—seriously.

Others use easily guessable authentication credentials like "admin:password" (yes, really).

● Susceptibility to Brute-Force Attacks

Many satellite communication systems rely on short keys that can be brute-forced in minutes or hours using modern GPUs or cloud computing.

Hackers can capture encrypted satellite signals and then use offline brute-force attacks to decrypt them at their leisure.

So, if an attacker wants to crack into a satellite system, they've got plenty of options.

Brute-Forcing Satellite Encryption: How Hackers Do It

Brute-forcing encryption means trying every possible key combination until you get the right one. And while that sounds time-consuming, modern computing power has made it shockingly fast.

Here's how hackers break satellite encryption step by step:

1️ Capturing Encrypted Signals

Hackers use Software-Defined Radios (SDRs) and satellite dish setups to record encrypted satellite transmissions.

These signals can be stored and analyzed later—no real-time attack needed.

2️ Identifying the Encryption Algorithm

Attackers analyze the signal's structure and metadata to determine what encryption method is being used.

If the system is using an outdated algorithm like DES, RC4, or weak AES, it's already game over.

3️ Dictionary and Rainbow Table Attacks

If the encryption relies on common or predictable keys, attackers use precomputed tables (rainbow tables) to crack it instantly.

Many satellite operators reuse encryption keys—meaning if one system is cracked, others using the same key are vulnerable too.

4️ Brute-Forcing with GPUs and Cloud Computing

Even strong encryption can be cracked if the key is too short.

Modern NVIDIA and AMD GPUs can try trillions of key combinations per second.

Attackers can rent cloud computing power from AWS, Google Cloud, or specialized brute-force services to accelerate cracking.

5️⃣ Decrypting and Manipulating Satellite Communications

Once the encryption is broken, attackers can read, alter, and even inject data into satellite transmissions.

Depending on the system, this could mean:

✅ Eavesdropping on sensitive data (military, financial, corporate secrets).

✅ Spoofing or modifying control signals (think hijacking drones or disrupting GPS).

✅ Taking over satellite uplinks (sending unauthorized commands to satellites).

Real-World Examples of Satellite Encryption Failures

🚀 Satellite TV Decryption (1990s - Present)

Hackers have been cracking and pirating satellite TV signals for decades.

Some providers used weak or no encryption, allowing people to watch premium channels for free.

Modern smart card systems fixed some issues, but pirates still find ways to bypass them.

📡 Global Navigation System Spoofing (2019)

Researchers demonstrated how weakly encrypted GPS signals could be brute-forced and manipulated.

Attackers could redirect ships and drones by injecting fake GPS data.

🔒 NASA Satellite Hacking (2008)

Chinese hackers allegedly took control of NASA Earth observation satellites by exploiting weak encryption in their communication protocols.

They interfered with satellite operations multiple times, proving how vulnerable some space assets really are.

These examples aren't just history lessons—they're warnings. If we don't fix satellite encryption weaknesses, hackers will continue exploiting them.

Defensive Measures: How to Protect Satellite Networks from Brute-Force Attacks

So, how do we stop hackers from brute-forcing satellite encryption like a cheap lock on a rusty bike?

✅ **Use Strong Encryption (AES-256, Post-Quantum Cryptography)**

Outdated encryption schemes like DES, RC4, and weak AES implementations must be replaced with AES-256 or post-quantum cryptographic algorithms.

Future satellites should adopt quantum-resistant encryption methods to prevent brute-force attacks from quantum computers.

✅ **Enforce Secure Key Management**

Encryption keys must be changed regularly and should never be hardcoded into satellite firmware.

Use hardware security modules (HSMs) and key rotation strategies to keep encryption keys safe.

✅ **Implement Strong Authentication**

Satellite uplink and downlink communications must use mutual authentication to prevent impersonation attacks.

Multi-factor authentication (MFA) should be enforced for ground station operators.

✅ **Use Frequency Hopping and Spread Spectrum Techniques**

Constantly changing frequencies makes it harder for attackers to capture and analyze encrypted signals.

This method is already used in military satellites but should be more widely adopted.

✓ Monitor and Detect Brute-Force Attempts

AI-based security systems should monitor unusual access attempts and brute-force activity on satellite networks.

Rate-limiting and intrusion detection can slow down or block brute-force attacks before they succeed.

Final Thoughts: Secure Your Satellites, or Someone Else Will

Brute-forcing and cracking weak encryption in satellite networks isn't some Hollywood cyber-thriller—it's happening right now.

The terrifying part? Many satellite systems still rely on outdated encryption that can be broken in minutes using modern computing power. If we don't start hardening encryption, improving authentication, and enforcing strong cybersecurity policies, we're just inviting attackers to take control of our space assets.

The good news? We can fix this. Stronger encryption, AI-based monitoring, and better key management can make it significantly harder for hackers to brute-force satellite networks.

But if we don't act fast? Well, let's just say your GPS might start telling you that your house is in the middle of the ocean, and your favorite TV satellite might start broadcasting nothing but hacker memes.

Secure your satellites. Or someone else will. 🚀

4.5 Securing Satellite Links from Unauthorized Access

Hackers in Space? Not on My Watch!

Look, I love a good sci-fi movie as much as the next person. But the idea of some basement hacker hijacking a satellite and demanding ransom isn't just fiction anymore—it's a real-world cybersecurity nightmare.

Satellites control everything from GPS navigation to military operations, and if an attacker gains access to these systems, things can go south—fast. Imagine a hacker redirecting commercial flights, disrupting emergency communications, or even turning off an entire country's internet. Yeah, not great.

The problem? Satellite links weren't built with today's cyber threats in mind. Many rely on outdated security, weak encryption, or even no authentication at all. The good news? We're not powerless. In this chapter, we'll break down how attackers breach satellite links and, more importantly, how we can stop them.

Understanding Satellite Links and Their Vulnerabilities

Satellite communication works through uplink and downlink channels:

Uplink (Earth → Satellite): The ground station or user terminal sends data to the satellite.

Downlink (Satellite → Earth): The satellite transmits data back to receivers on the ground.

To secure these links, we need to understand the common weaknesses that attackers exploit:

● **Weak or No Encryption**

Some satellites still use outdated encryption methods (like DES or weak AES).

Others don't encrypt their signals at all, making them easy to intercept.

● **Lack of Authentication**

Many satellites don't verify who's sending them commands, meaning anyone with the right equipment could potentially send instructions.

Some older satellites use default credentials (hello, "admin/admin" disasters).

● **Jamming and Spoofing Attacks**

Attackers can jam satellite signals, preventing legitimate communication.

Spoofers can inject fake signals to manipulate data or deceive receivers (think GPS spoofing).

● Replay and Man-in-the-Middle (MITM) Attacks

Hackers can capture legitimate transmissions and replay them later to take control.

MITM attacks allow an attacker to intercept and modify data in transit.

With these risks in mind, let's talk about how we can actually protect satellite links from unauthorized access.

Securing Uplink Communications: Stopping Unauthorized Commands

The uplink is the most critical part of a satellite system—because if an attacker takes control here, they can issue commands to the satellite itself. Here's how we secure it:

✅ Strong Encryption (AES-256 and Beyond)

Use AES-256 or post-quantum encryption for all uplink commands.

Any weak encryption should be phased out immediately.

✅ Multi-Factor Authentication (MFA) for Ground Stations

Require multiple authentication factors before a ground station can send commands.

Use biometric access, hardware tokens, or cryptographic authentication.

✅ Command Whitelisting

Satellites should have a pre-approved list of valid commands.

Any unexpected or unauthorized command should be automatically rejected.

✅ Anti-Replay Protection

Use one-time authentication tokens or time-based challenges to prevent replay attacks.

Ensure that each command has a unique cryptographic nonce.

✅ Frequency Hopping for Secure Uplink

Rapidly changing frequencies makes it harder for attackers to capture or jam uplink signals.

This is already used in military satellites but should be expanded to commercial and IoT satellites.

Securing Downlink Communications: Preventing Eavesdropping

Even if an attacker can't send commands to a satellite, they might still intercept its data. Here's how we lock down the downlink:

✅ End-to-End Encryption

Every piece of data transmitted should be encrypted—whether it's GPS coordinates, financial transactions, or internet traffic.

Zero-trust encryption ensures that even if an attacker intercepts the transmission, they can't read or modify it.

✅ Geofencing and Access Control

Restrict satellite downlink transmissions only to authorized regions.

Use whitelisted IP ranges and secure VPNs for receiving satellite data.

✅ Tamper-Detection Mechanisms

Implement AI-driven anomaly detection to monitor for unauthorized access.

Any unusual signal interception attempts should trigger an alert.

✅ Quantum Cryptography for Future-Proof Security

Traditional encryption methods are at risk from quantum computing in the near future.

Quantum key distribution (QKD) ensures that encryption keys are safe even from advanced quantum attacks.

Defensive Strategies: Hardening Satellite Communications

To secure both uplink and downlink communications, we need a layered defense approach:

✅ AI-Powered Intrusion Detection Systems (IDS)

AI-driven security can detect and mitigate unauthorized access in real-time.

Machine learning can recognize unusual patterns and shut down anomalous activities before they escalate.

✅ Red Team Testing for Space Systems

Regular penetration testing is crucial to identify weaknesses before attackers do.

Simulated attacks help uncover vulnerabilities in encryption, authentication, and signal integrity.

✅ Updating Satellite Firmware and Security Protocols

Regular updates can patch vulnerabilities and strengthen encryption.

Satellites should have a secure firmware update mechanism to prevent malicious updates.

✅ Building Redundancy into Satellite Systems

Backup satellites and alternative communication channels ensure that attacks on one system don't cause a total failure.

Redundancy prevents catastrophic service disruptions.

The Future of Securing Satellite Links: What's Next?

As hackers evolve, so must our defenses. The future of securing satellite communications includes:

🚀 **Post-Quantum Cryptography** – Protecting satellites from quantum-based attacks.

🚀 **Blockchain for Secure Communications** – Decentralized security for space systems.

🚀 **AI-Driven Autonomous Defense** – Machine learning that can detect and counteract attacks in real time.

🚀 **Stronger International Regulations** – Global enforcement of secure satellite communication standards.

Final Thoughts: Lock Down Your Satellites Before Hackers Do

If satellites are the backbone of modern communication, then securing their links should be priority #1. Yet, many space systems still operate with outdated encryption, weak authentication, and almost no real-time security monitoring.

The takeaway? Hackers are watching. If we don't start taking satellite cybersecurity seriously, they'll continue exploiting these weaknesses.

The good news? We can lock down our satellites with better encryption, smarter authentication, and AI-driven defenses. But we need to act fast—before the next big satellite hack makes headlines.

Because let's be real—no one wants to wake up and find out their GPS is sending them to Mars instead of Starbucks. 🚀

Chapter 5: GPS and GNSS Spoofing Attacks

Ever wanted to convince your phone that you're in Paris while sitting in your underwear at home? Well, GPS spoofing can do that—except hackers use it for way more devious things, like rerouting ships, misleading aircraft, and even tricking autonomous vehicles. With a bit of SDR magic, you can make a GPS receiver believe it's literally anywhere on Earth (or off it).

This chapter covers the fundamentals of Global Navigation Satellite Systems (GNSS), including GPS, Galileo, GLONASS, and BeiDou. We'll explore tools like HackRF and BladeRF for GPS spoofing, case studies of real-world GPS manipulation incidents, and, most importantly, the defensive measures used to protect navigation systems from these attacks.

5.1 Understanding GPS, Galileo, GLONASS, and BeiDou Navigation Systems

Lost in Space? Not Anymore (Unless a Hacker Gets Involved)

Ever had your GPS send you to the middle of nowhere when you were just trying to find the nearest coffee shop? Imagine that, but on a global scale—airplanes, ships, and even entire military operations depending on satellite navigation. If that system goes haywire, we're not just missing exits on the freeway—we're talking about economic chaos, compromised security, and even life-threatening situations.

Navigation satellites are the backbone of modern positioning systems, powering everything from your phone's Google Maps to precision missile guidance systems. And guess what? They're not just one system—there's a whole network of global navigation satellite systems (GNSS), each operated by different countries, each with their own quirks, advantages, and, of course, vulnerabilities.

So, before we dive into hacking and securing GPS, let's break down the four major GNSS systems—because knowing how they work is the first step in understanding how attackers exploit them.

What is GNSS?

GNSS, or Global Navigation Satellite System, is an umbrella term for any satellite-based positioning system. These systems provide real-time location, velocity, and time data to receivers worldwide. Currently, four major GNSS exist:

GPS (United States)

Galileo (European Union)

GLONASS (Russia)

BeiDou (China)

Each of these systems has its own set of satellites, frequencies, and operational protocols, but they all share a common goal: helping you (and global industries) know exactly where you are.

1. GPS (Global Positioning System - USA)

✓ **Operator**: United States Government
✓ **Satellites in Orbit**: ~31 operational satellites
✓ **Accuracy**: Civilian (5-10 meters), Military (centimeter-level with encrypted signals)
✓ **Frequencies**: L1, L2, L5

Developed by the U.S. Department of Defense (DoD) in the 1970s, GPS was originally built for military use but was later opened up for civilian applications. It consists of 31 satellites orbiting at an altitude of 20,200 km, broadcasting signals that allow devices to triangulate their location.

GPS works on a trilateration method—your device picks up signals from at least four satellites, calculates the signal travel time, and determines your precise location.

● Weaknesses and Vulnerabilities:

Easily jammed with high-power interference.

Spoofable—attackers can transmit fake GPS signals to deceive receivers.

Relies on a single country's control (which means geopolitical risks if access is restricted).

2. Galileo (European Union's GNSS)

✅ **Operator**: European Space Agency (ESA)

✅ **Satellites in Orbit**: 30 (24 operational, 6 spares)

✅ **Accuracy**: Civilian (~1 meter), PRS (military-grade) ~20 cm

✅ **Frequencies**: E1, E5a, E5b, E6

Galileo is the EU's answer to GPS—a high-accuracy GNSS designed to reduce reliance on American-controlled systems. It provides open, commercial, and encrypted government signals, with an accuracy of up to 20 cm for authorized users (way better than standard GPS).

One of Galileo's big advantages? It's designed to be more resistant to jamming and spoofing attacks. It also operates at a higher frequency, allowing better signal penetration in urban areas and difficult terrains.

⬤ **Weaknesses and Vulnerabilities:**

Still dependent on U.S. GPS for full interoperability.

Faces cybersecurity risks due to its extensive network of ground control stations.

3. GLONASS (Russia's GNSS)

✅ **Operator**: Russian Space Agency

✅ **Satellites in Orbit**: 24 operational

✅ **Accuracy**: Civilian (5-10 meters), Military (sub-meter)

✅ **Frequencies**: L1, L2, L3

GLONASS was developed by Russia during the Cold War as an alternative to GPS. While its accuracy is comparable to GPS, its primary strength lies in better coverage at high latitudes, meaning it performs well in Russia's northern regions where GPS signals struggle.

⬤ **Weaknesses and Vulnerabilities:**

Lower satellite lifespan compared to GPS and Galileo.

Historically faced funding issues, leading to occasional gaps in service.

Some GLONASS signals have been reported to be more susceptible to jamming.

4. BeiDou (China's GNSS)

✅ **Operator**: China National Space Administration (CNSA)
✅ **Satellites in Orbit**: 45+ operational satellites
✅ **Accuracy**: Civilian (5-10 meters), Encrypted (centimeter-level)
✅ **Frequencies**: B1, B2, B3

BeiDou is China's independent navigation system, built to reduce reliance on GPS. What makes BeiDou unique is its two-way communication capability—unlike GPS, which only sends signals one way, BeiDou allows users to send short messages back to satellites, making it useful for emergency situations.

● **Weaknesses and Vulnerabilities:**

Heavily dependent on Chinese government control.

Two-way communication opens up potential security risks.

Not yet as widely adopted as GPS or Galileo outside of China.

Comparing GPS, Galileo, GLONASS, and BeiDou

Feature	GPS (USA)	Galileo (EU)	GLONASS (Russia)	BeiDou (China)
Satellites	31	30	24	45+
Operator	US DoD	European Space Agency	Russian Space Agency	CNSA
Civilian Accuracy	5-10m	~1m	5-10m	5-10m
Military Accuracy	Sub-meter	20 cm	Sub-meter	Centimeter-level
Best Feature	Global coverage	High accuracy	Works well at high latitudes	Two-way communication
Weakness	Easily spoofed/jammed	Still interoperates with GPS	Older satellites, easier to jam	Government-controlled

Final Thoughts: Why GNSS Security Matters

We live in a world where everything from Google Maps to military operations depends on satellite navigation. A single spoofing attack could misdirect ships, planes, or emergency responders. A nation-state jamming GPS could disrupt an entire economy.

Hackers aren't just targeting your Wi-Fi anymore—they're looking to the skies. In the next sections, we'll dive into how attackers can spoof GPS signals and how we can defend against satellite navigation hacks.

Because the last thing we need is hackers sending us all in the wrong direction—literally. 🚀

5.2 Tools and Techniques for GPS Spoofing (HackRF, BladeRF, SDR Kits)

Lost? Or Just Spoofed?

Ever had Google Maps tell you to turn right into a lake? Or found yourself inexplicably 500 miles away from your actual location on a tracking app? Well, before you blame your phone's GPS, consider this—you might have been spoofed.

GPS spoofing is every navigator's worst nightmare—it's when an attacker transmits fake GPS signals to deceive a receiver into thinking it's somewhere it's not. Sounds like a plot from a spy movie, right? But it's real. And surprisingly easy to do with the right tools.

In this chapter, we'll explore the weapons of choice for GPS spoofing—HackRF, BladeRF, and SDR kits—and how attackers (and security researchers) use them to manipulate location data.

What is GPS Spoofing?
GPS spoofing is the art of faking satellite signals to mislead receivers. Instead of blocking signals like GPS jamming, spoofing tricks devices into believing a fabricated location—meaning ships, drones, cars, and even people can be misdirected without realizing it.

◆ **Common uses of GPS spoofing (both good and bad):**

Hacking navigation systems (misdirecting drones, self-driving cars, or even aircraft).

Protecting privacy (fooling location-tracking apps).

Bypassing geofencing restrictions (cheating in location-based games like Pokémon GO).

Cyberwarfare & military deception (misleading enemy forces or interfering with missile guidance).

Essential Tools for GPS Spoofing

Now, let's talk about the tools of the trade—radio hardware and software that allow attackers and researchers to manipulate GPS signals.

1. HackRF One – The Budget-Friendly GPS Spoofer

- **Price**: ~$300
- **Type**: Software-defined radio (SDR)
- **Frequency Range**: 1 MHz to 6 GHz
- **Ideal For**: Beginners in GPS spoofing

HackRF One is an affordable and versatile SDR that can transmit and receive radio signals, making it a great choice for low-cost GPS spoofing experiments. It's popular among ethical hackers, security researchers, and cybercriminals alike due to its open-source software compatibility (GNU Radio, SDR#).

● **Limitations:**

Limited to single-band transmission (can't spoof multi-frequency GPS signals).

Low power output, meaning it can only spoof short-range devices (like a phone or drone within a few meters).

2. BladeRF – The Professional's Choice

- **Price**: ~$650
- **Type**: High-performance SDR
- **Frequency Range**: 300 MHz to 3.8 GHz
- **Ideal For**: Intermediate & advanced attackers

BladeRF is a step up from HackRF, offering full-duplex (simultaneous transmission & reception), better frequency stability, and more power—meaning you can spoof GPS signals over longer distances.

● **Limitations**:

Higher cost makes it less accessible for beginners.

Requires more technical expertise than HackRF.

3. Ettus USRP (Universal Software Radio Peripheral) – The Military-Grade Beast

◆ **Price**: $1,000 - $10,000+
◆ **Type**: Advanced SDR for professional research
◆ **Frequency Range**: Configurable (can handle L1/L2 GPS frequencies)
◆ **Ideal For**: Government, military, and serious cyber researchers

Ettus USRP is the gold standard for professionals in government labs and defense agencies. It supports multiple GPS frequency bands, making it powerful enough to spoof military-grade navigation systems (not just civilian GPS).

● **Limitations**:

Extremely expensive for personal use.

Highly regulated (buying one can raise red flags if you're not a legitimate researcher).

Software for GPS Spoofing

Hardware alone isn't enough—you need software to generate and manipulate fake GPS signals. Here are some of the most widely used tools:

1. GPS-SDR-SIM

✓ Open-source GPS signal simulator

✓ Works with HackRF & BladeRF

✓ Can generate custom fake GPS signals

This tool allows you to simulate GPS signals from anywhere in the world—whether that's moving a drone over the White House (not recommended) or teleporting your car to another continent (also not recommended).

2. GNSS-SDR

✅ Professional-grade GPS signal processing software

✅ Used for both spoofing and defending against GPS attacks

✅ Compatible with advanced SDR hardware like USRP

GNSS-SDR is used in academic and military research to analyze real-time GPS signals—it's a powerful tool, but it requires deep technical knowledge to operate.

Techniques for GPS Spoofing

So, how do attackers actually deploy GPS spoofing? Here's a simplified breakdown:

1. Record and Replay Attacks (RRA)

🎯 **Attack Strategy**: Record real GPS signals and replay them at a different location.
♦ **Pros**: Simple and effective.
♦ **Cons**: Can only trick devices into believing they are at a previously recorded location.

2. Synthetic GPS Spoofing

🎯 **Attack Strategy**: Generate entirely new GPS signals using software like GPS-SDR-SIM.
♦ **Pros**: More advanced—allows for dynamic control of location.
♦ **Cons**: Requires precise synchronization with real satellites.

3. Meaconing (Delay Spoofing)

🎯 **Attack Strategy**: Capture and rebroadcast real GPS signals with a delay.
♦ **Pros**: Harder to detect because it doesn't completely replace signals.
♦ **Cons**: Only works for short-range targets (e.g., nearby drones, vehicles).

Defensive Measures Against GPS Spoofing

Before you panic and throw your GPS device in the trash, let's talk about how to defend against spoofing attacks:

◈ **Multi-frequency & multi-GNSS receivers** (Using Galileo + GPS + GLONASS makes spoofing harder).
◈ **Cryptographic authentication** (New GPS signals, like GPS L5 and Galileo OS-NMA, include security features).
◈ **Anti-spoofing AI & anomaly detection** (Some advanced systems use machine learning to detect fake signals).
◈ **INS (Inertial Navigation Systems) as a backup** (Planes, ships, and military vehicles use gyroscopes & accelerometers to cross-check GPS data).

Final Thoughts: GPS Spoofing is No Joke

GPS spoofing isn't just some tech prank—it's a real threat that can cause planes to go off course, ships to stray into hostile waters, and self-driving cars to drive into walls. The tools and techniques we've discussed here are widely available, and bad actors are already using them.

But don't worry—just because hackers can spoof your location doesn't mean you're defenseless. By understanding how GPS spoofing works, we can build better security defenses to keep our satellite navigation systems reliable and trustworthy.

After all, getting lost is bad enough. Getting deliberately misled by a hacker? Now, that's just rude. 🚀

5.3 Creating Fake Navigation Data to Mislead Satellites and Ground Systems

Lost in Space… on Purpose

Imagine this: You're on a road trip, following GPS directions, and suddenly your map tells you that you've arrived at your destination—in the middle of the ocean. Your car is very much on solid ground, but your GPS thinks you just drove into Atlantis.

Congratulations, you've just been spoofed.

While this might sound like a minor inconvenience for a road trip, in the wrong hands, fake navigation data can wreak havoc on ships, aircraft, military assets, and even financial systems that rely on precise timing from GPS signals. In this chapter, we'll explore how attackers generate fake navigation data to deceive satellites and ground-based receivers—and, more importantly, how to defend against these deceptions.

How Fake Navigation Data Works

At its core, GPS and GNSS systems (Global Navigation Satellite Systems) rely on signals from multiple satellites to determine location and time. These signals contain highly accurate timing and positioning data that receivers (like your phone, a ship's navigation system, or a military drone) use to calculate their exact position on Earth.

Fake navigation data attacks work by sending manipulated signals to fool receivers into calculating the wrong location or time. This can be done in multiple ways:

◆ GPS Spoofing: Broadcasting fake GNSS signals to mislead receivers.
◆ Data Injection: Modifying or corrupting navigation data in transit.
◆ Clock Manipulation: Changing timing data to disrupt financial or military systems.

Now, let's break down how attackers create fake navigation data and inject it into real-world systems.

Step 1: Choosing the Right Tools for the Job

Creating fake navigation data requires specialized hardware and software, typically found in cybersecurity research labs, military operations, or underground hacker forums. Here are the most common tools:

1. Software-Defined Radios (SDRs)

HackRF One, BladeRF, and Ettus USRP are the go-to SDRs for GPS manipulation. These devices can transmit and receive radio signals, making them perfect for generating fake GPS or GNSS signals.

◆ **HackRF One** – Affordable and widely used, but limited in range.
◆ **BladeRF** – More powerful, supports full-duplex transmission.
◆ **Ettus USRP** – Military-grade, capable of spoofing high-precision GPS systems.

2. GPS Signal Simulators

Specialized GPS simulation software allows attackers to generate and control fake satellite signals. Some popular options include:

✓ **GPS-SDR-SIM** – Open-source tool for generating fake GPS signals.

✓ **GNSS-SDR** – More advanced, supports multiple satellite constellations (GPS, Galileo, BeiDou, GLONASS).

✓ **Skydel** – Professional-grade GPS simulator used in defense and aerospace industries.

3. GNSS Signal Replay Tools

Attackers can record real GPS signals and then play them back to trick receivers. This method, called meaconing, is used to shift locations subtly without raising alarms.

◆ **RTL-SDR + GNURadio** – Popular for signal replay attacks.

◆ **Open-source Python scripts** – Custom tools for modifying and replaying GPS data.

Step 2: Generating Fake GPS Signals

Once an attacker has the necessary tools, the next step is creating a convincing fake navigation signal. There are three main ways to do this:

1. Basic Location Spoofing

🎯 **Goal**: Trick a GPS receiver into thinking it's somewhere else.

An attacker transmits fake GNSS signals using an SDR, making the target believe it's in a different location. This method is used to:

Bypass geofencing (e.g., faking a location to access region-locked content).

Misdirect vehicles or drones (e.g., causing a drone to land in the wrong location).

Disrupt fleet tracking systems (e.g., making a stolen truck appear to be on its planned route).

2. Dynamic Navigation Manipulation

🎯 **Goal**: Simulate movement to create a believable false trajectory.

Instead of just faking a static position, attackers generate a moving GPS path that appears legitimate to navigation systems. This is useful for:

Making a hijacked ship appear to be on course while it's actually heading to a pirate-controlled location.

Causing an aircraft autopilot system to drift off course.

Confusing surveillance systems by creating fake vehicle movement patterns.

3. Time Synchronization Attacks

🎯 **Goal**: Disrupt systems that rely on precise GPS timing.

GPS signals don't just provide location data—they also serve as a global time reference for:

Financial markets (stock trading timestamps).

Military operations (synchronized attacks).

Power grids (timing signals for electricity distribution).

By manipulating GPS timing signals, attackers can cause serious disruptions. Imagine Wall Street losing precise timestamps—billions could be lost in milliseconds.

Real-World GPS Spoofing Incidents

GPS spoofing isn't just a theoretical attack—it's been used by nation-states, criminals, and researchers in high-profile incidents:

● **2019 - Iran Spoofs a U.S. Drone**

Iranian forces allegedly spoofed a U.S. RQ-170 drone's GPS signals, tricking it into landing in an Iranian airbase instead of its intended destination.

● **2021 - Maritime Spoofing in the Black Sea**

Multiple ships in the Black Sea reported fake GPS locations, making them appear to be miles away from their actual positions. This is suspected to be a nation-state attack on commercial and military vessels.

● **Pokémon GO Spoofers (2016 - Present)**

Players have been using GPS spoofing to fake locations and collect rare Pokémon from around the world without leaving their couch.

How to Defend Against Fake Navigation Data Attacks

Fortunately, researchers and engineers have developed countermeasures to detect and prevent GPS spoofing. Here are some effective defenses:

1. Multi-GNSS Systems

Instead of relying on just GPS, modern receivers use multiple GNSS constellations (Galileo, GLONASS, BeiDou) to cross-check locations.

2. Signal Authentication

Newer navigation systems (e.g., Galileo OS-NMA) use cryptographic authentication to verify signal integrity.

3. AI-Powered Spoofing Detection

Machine learning algorithms analyze GPS anomalies to detect fake signals in real time.

4. Inertial Navigation Systems (INS)

Aircraft and ships use INS sensors (gyroscopes, accelerometers) to track motion independently of GPS—making spoofing harder.

Final Thoughts: Can You Trust Your GPS?

In today's world, where everything from Uber rides to missile guidance systems relies on GPS, fake navigation data is a real threat. And while security measures are improving, attackers are constantly finding new ways to deceive systems.

So, next time your GPS tells you to turn left into a brick wall, remember—it might not be a bug. It could be someone having a little too much fun with a HackRF One. 🚀

5.4 Case Studies: Real-World GPS Spoofing Incidents and Their Impact

When Your GPS Lies to You… and It's Not a Software Bug

Ever been driving, following your GPS, and suddenly it tells you to make a U-turn in the middle of a highway? Or that you've arrived at your destination… which happens to be a lake? Now, imagine that happening on a global scale—but with military drones, cargo ships, and commercial airplanes.

GPS spoofing isn't just a fun prank or a way for lazy gamers to fake their Pokémon GO location. It's a high-stakes cybersecurity threat with real-world consequences—from ships veering off course to multi-million-dollar drones being hijacked. In this chapter, we'll dive into real cases of GPS spoofing, who did it, why, and what kind of chaos followed.

Case Study #1: Iran's Capture of a U.S. Military Drone (2011)

What Happened?

In December 2011, the U.S. military lost control of an RQ-170 Sentinel drone over Afghanistan. Strangely, the drone didn't crash—it landed perfectly intact inside Iran. The Iranian military claimed they had successfully hijacked the drone using GPS spoofing.

How Did They Do It?

The theory is that Iranian cyberwarfare experts spoofed weak GPS signals, tricking the drone into thinking it was approaching a friendly base instead of enemy territory. Since many drones rely on GPS for navigation, the fake signals led the drone to land at an Iranian-controlled airstrip instead of returning to its base.

Impact & Consequences

✅ The U.S. lost a top-secret stealth drone worth over $6 million.

✅ Iran reverse-engineered the drone's technology and later showcased their own "copy."

✅ This incident led the U.S. military to improve anti-spoofing technologies in drones.

Case Study #2: The Black Sea Ship Spoofing Mystery (2017 & 2021)

What Happened?

In 2017, multiple ships navigating the Black Sea reported a bizarre problem: their GPS systems suddenly placed them at an airport miles inland, rather than at sea.

A similar incident happened again in 2021. Cargo ships and tankers operating near Russia's waters reported GPS locations that didn't match reality, causing confusion in maritime navigation systems.

How Did It Happen?

Investigators believe this was a nation-state GPS spoofing attack, likely conducted by Russia to protect strategic areas or disrupt foreign intelligence gathering. The fake GPS signals tricked ship navigation systems, making them believe they were in a completely different location.

Impact & Consequences

✅ Maritime navigation was disrupted, leading to delays and risks of ship collisions.

✅ It highlighted vulnerabilities in global shipping and trade security.

✅ Russia was suspected of testing electronic warfare capabilities.

Case Study #3: China's "Ghost Ships" Spoofing (2019 - Present)

What Happened?

A large number of ships near Chinese ports suddenly appeared to be "jumping" to random locations, including moving in impossible patterns or showing up miles away from their actual locations.

How Did It Happen?

Experts believe this is deliberate GPS spoofing being used by Chinese authorities to:

Conceal sensitive military movements.

Disrupt foreign tracking of Chinese vessels.

Create "ghost ships" that appear on tracking systems but don't actually exist.

Impact & Consequences

✓ International shipping and port operations were heavily disrupted.

✓ Intelligence agencies had difficulty tracking real Chinese military activities.

✓ The incident exposed how easy it is to manipulate GPS tracking on a global scale.

Case Study #4: The Moscow Taxi GPS Anomaly (2016 - Present)

What Happened?

Ever tried using Uber in Moscow's Red Square, only to find that your app thinks you're at the airport? Well, you're not alone.

For years, GPS systems near the Kremlin have been spoofed, making it nearly impossible to get accurate location data within certain zones.

How Did It Happen?

Russia appears to be using localized GPS spoofing as a security measure to protect high-profile locations like:

The Kremlin (to prevent drone attacks or surveillance).

Government buildings (to block GPS-guided espionage tools).

Military bases (to prevent tracking of movements).

Impact & Consequences

✓ Taxis and delivery services get sent to the wrong locations.

✓ Drones and navigation apps fail near critical sites.

☑ It showcases how GPS spoofing is used as a defensive tool by governments.

Case Study #5: Pokémon GO Spoofing (2016 - Present)

What Happened?

Not all GPS spoofing is about military drones and global espionage. When Pokémon GO launched in 2016, some players realized they didn't actually have to go outside to catch Pokémon. Instead, they used GPS spoofing to make their phones appear anywhere in the world.

How Did It Happen?

Players used:

☑ Fake GPS apps on Android & iOS to teleport to rare Pokémon locations.

☑ SDR tools to spoof signals and trick their phones.

☑ VPNs and proxies to bypass location checks.

Impact & Consequences

☑ Players cheated their way to rare Pokémon without leaving home.

☑ Niantic (Pokémon GO's creator) implemented anti-spoofing measures, banning thousands of accounts.

☑ This exposed the real-world ease of GPS spoofing, leading to improved detection techniques in cybersecurity.

Lessons Learned: The Dangers of GPS Spoofing

GPS spoofing isn't just a theoretical cybersecurity risk—it's an active threat that governments, militaries, and even regular citizens are dealing with every day. From drone hijackings to manipulating global trade, fake GPS signals have real-world consequences.

Key Takeaways from These Case Studies:

✅ Nation-states actively use GPS spoofing for defense and cyberwarfare.

✅ Maritime and aviation industries are vulnerable to GPS manipulation.

✅ Spoofing is surprisingly easy with off-the-shelf SDR tools.

✅ Security measures like multi-GNSS verification and AI-based anomaly detection are improving defenses.

Final Thought: Can You Trust Your GPS?

Next time you're lost and your GPS seems a little... off—consider the possibility that someone, somewhere, might be having fun with a spoofing tool. 😼

5.5 Defensive Measures Against GNSS Spoofing and Navigation Attacks

Protecting Your GPS: Because Getting Lost Should Be Your Own Fault

We've all been there—one minute you're following your GPS like a loyal minion, and the next, it's confidently directing you to take a right turn… into a lake. But while a bad GPS signal can be annoying for your weekend road trip, GNSS spoofing is a serious security risk that can lead to hijacked drones, lost cargo ships, and planes flying off-course.

So, how do we stop the bad guys from tricking our GPS? Well, you can't exactly punch a spoofing attack in the face, but you can outsmart it. In this chapter, we'll explore cutting-edge defenses against GNSS spoofing and how governments, military agencies, and even everyday users can keep their navigation systems from being fooled.

1. Multi-GNSS Verification: The "Trust, but Verify" Approach

One of the simplest ways to defend against GPS spoofing is to use multiple satellite navigation systems instead of relying on just one. The major GNSS constellations—GPS (USA), Galileo (EU), GLONASS (Russia), and BeiDou (China)—all provide separate signals.

Why This Works:

- A spoofer would need to manipulate multiple GNSS signals simultaneously, which is significantly harder.
- If one system starts acting weird, a device can compare it to others and detect inconsistencies.
- Some high-security applications now require multi-GNSS checks to validate location accuracy.

2. Signal Authentication: Teaching GPS to Recognize a Fake

GPS was originally built without authentication, meaning anyone can broadcast fake signals that look legitimate. However, modern GNSS advancements have started introducing cryptographic authentication methods to verify signal integrity.

Authentication Methods:

- **Navigation Message Authentication (NMA):** Encrypts GNSS signals so receivers can verify legitimacy.
- **Spreading Code Authentication**: Helps receivers differentiate real signals from spoofed ones.
- **CHIMERA (Chip-Scale Atomic Clock Authentication):** A next-gen technology for GPS signal validation.

Fun Fact: Galileo is currently the only GNSS system that fully supports cryptographic authentication in civilian signals!

3. Anti-Spoofing Antennas: Smart Hardware for Smart Defenses

Most GNSS spoofing attacks work by overpowering real satellite signals with stronger fake ones. But anti-spoofing antennas can help mitigate this by filtering and detecting inconsistencies in signal sources.

Types of Anti-Spoofing Antennas:

- **Directional Antennas**: Only accept signals from known satellite positions.
- **Dual-Polarized Antennas**: Help identify spoofed signals based on polarization.
- **Null-Steering Antennas**: Actively block signals that don't align with expected locations.

Best for: Military aircraft, critical infrastructure, and high-security applications.

4. Machine Learning-Based Spoofing Detection: AI to the Rescue!

Cybercriminals are getting smarter, but so is AI. Machine learning algorithms can analyze GNSS signals in real-time, detecting abnormalities that humans might miss.

How AI Helps:

- **Anomaly Detection**: Flags suspicious signal behavior.
- **Pattern Recognition**: Learns normal GNSS signal patterns and detects deviations.
- **Adaptive Filtering**: Helps dynamically adjust navigation data when spoofing is detected.

Who's Using This? The U.S. Air Force, major aviation companies, and even autonomous vehicle manufacturers are integrating AI-driven GNSS protection!

5. Inertial Navigation Systems (INS): The Backup Plan

A solid defense against GPS spoofing is to not rely on GPS at all. Enter Inertial Navigation Systems (INS)—a technology that allows aircraft, ships, and vehicles to navigate without GNSS signals.

How INS Works:

- Uses gyroscopes, accelerometers, and magnetometers to track movement.
- Provides short-term navigation without external signals.
- Often used in submarines, fighter jets, and spacecraft.

Best for: Military operations, self-driving cars, and any high-security system that can't afford GPS failures.

6. Time Synchronization with Atomic Clocks: The Ultimate GPS Lie Detector

Since GPS spoofing works by manipulating timing signals, using atomic clocks can help detect fake signals. If a spoofed GPS signal provides a different timestamp than the atomic clock, the system can flag it as suspicious.

Why Atomic Clocks Work:

- They are ultra-precise—accurate to one second in millions of years.

- They provide an independent time source to cross-check GPS timestamps.
- Many high-security networks already use them to verify GNSS reliability.

Used in: Financial systems, military applications, and even power grids to ensure time-based security.

7. Jamming Detection & Adaptive Filtering: The Cybersecurity Firewall for GNSS

Some GNSS security solutions focus on detecting jamming or signal anomalies before they escalate into a full-blown spoofing attack.

- **Jamming Detectors**: Identify areas where GNSS signals are being blocked.
- **Adaptive Filtering**: Helps clean up spoofed signals by analyzing unexpected shifts in frequency or power levels.
- **Geo-Fencing & Alerts**: Notifies users when their GNSS signals suddenly jump to a different location.

Example: Many high-security airports and military bases have jamming detection to protect against GPS disruptions.

Conclusion: Defending Your GPS Like a Pro

Spoofing attacks are getting more sophisticated every year, but so are our defenses. The key takeaway? Relying on GPS alone is risky. Whether it's a military drone, a commercial aircraft, or just your Uber ride—having multiple layers of security is the only way to ensure that when your GPS says you're home, you're not actually in the middle of the ocean.

Top Defensive Strategies Against GNSS Spoofing:

- Use Multi-GNSS (GPS, Galileo, GLONASS, BeiDou).
- Enable cryptographic authentication for GPS signals.
- Use anti-spoofing antennas and machine learning detection.
- Integrate Inertial Navigation Systems (INS) as a backup.
- Cross-check time signals with atomic clocks.
- Deploy jam detection & adaptive filtering for early warnings.

Final Thought: Because Getting Lost Should Be an Honest Mistake

We've all had bad GPS days, but at least now you know that when your navigation system freaks out, it might not be your phone—it could be a full-scale cyberwarfare attack happening in real-time.

So, the next time your GPS says you're in the middle of the Atlantic Ocean, maybe… just maybe… check another source before calling the Coast Guard.

Chapter 6: Jamming and Denial-of-Service Attacks on Satellites

Ever had your Wi-Fi slow to a crawl just because your neighbor decided to microwave some leftovers? Now imagine that—but on a global scale. Satellite jamming is like the cosmic version of throwing a wrench into the gears of global communication, and attackers have been using it for years to disrupt everything from GPS to military operations.

This chapter explores the principles of RF jamming, uplink and downlink attacks, and Distributed Denial-of-Service (DDoS) strategies targeting satellite networks. We'll also examine cases of electromagnetic interference (EMI) and cyber-physical attacks, along with mitigation techniques designed to ensure the resilience of space-based systems.

6.1 Basics of RF Jamming and Its Effects on Satellite Communications

Jamming 101: Because Sometimes, Satellites Just Want to Ghost You

Ever had that moment where your Wi-Fi cuts out right before you hit "Submit" on an important email? Or when your GPS suddenly stops working, leaving you stranded in the middle of nowhere? Now, imagine that happening to an entire country's military, aviation, or emergency response system. That, my friends, is the magic (or nightmare) of radio frequency (RF) jamming—the cybersecurity equivalent of stuffing a sock in someone's mouth while they're trying to talk.

RF jamming is one of the simplest, yet most brutally effective, ways to disrupt satellite communications. Whether you're a government trying to block enemy transmissions, a hacker testing vulnerabilities, or just a guy with a questionable moral compass and a high-powered transmitter, jamming can render satellites temporarily useless. In this section, we'll break down how jamming works, why it's a huge problem for satellite networks, and how to fight back against the digital silence.

1. What is RF Jamming?

At its core, RF jamming is intentional interference with radio signals, flooding the airwaves with noise so that legitimate communications can't get through. Think of it like trying to have a conversation at a rock concert—the background noise drowns out your voice, making it impossible for anyone to understand what you're saying.

Types of RF Jamming:

- **Spot Jamming** – Targets a specific frequency, disrupting only one type of signal.
- **Sweep Jamming** – Rapidly moves across multiple frequencies, blocking multiple signals.
- **Barrage Jamming** – Blasts a wide range of frequencies all at once, causing massive disruption.
- **Smart Jamming** – Uses AI or advanced algorithms to selectively jam specific signals while leaving others intact.

2. How Does Jamming Affect Satellite Communications?

Satellites are particularly vulnerable to jamming because they rely on weak signals traveling vast distances from space to Earth. Even a relatively low-powered ground-based jammer can overwhelm these signals, leading to:

- **Loss of GPS Navigation** – Aircraft, ships, and even self-driving cars could be left directionless.
- **Communication Blackouts** – Emergency services, military units, and businesses lose satellite links.
- **Interference in Military Operations** – Disrupts drone strikes, missile guidance, and encrypted messaging.
- **Disrupted Financial & Internet Services** – Many financial transactions rely on precise satellite timing.

Real-World Example: In 2011, North Korea reportedly jammed GPS signals over Seoul, affecting flights, ships, and critical infrastructure.

3. Who Uses Jamming, and Why?

While jamming is illegal in most cases, governments, criminals, and even pranksters have all found ways to exploit it:

- **Military & Intelligence Agencies** – Used for electronic warfare to disrupt enemy communications.
- **Hackers & Cybercriminals** – Used to interfere with GPS tracking or hijack satellite signals.

- **Corporations & Nation-States** – Used in trade wars or geopolitical conflicts to control information flow.
- **Black Market & Smugglers** – Used to evade law enforcement tracking via GPS jammers.

4. How is RF Jamming Performed?

Jamming a satellite isn't as hard as you'd think. In fact, with the right equipment, it can be done from a van in a parking lot (but don't get any ideas).

Basic Steps of a Jamming Attack:

- **Identify Target Frequencies** – Find out which frequencies the satellite operates on (L-band for GPS, C-band for some comms, etc.).
- **Generate a High-Powered RF Signal** – Use a signal generator, software-defined radio (SDR), or modified radio transmitter.
- **Transmit Interference at the Right Frequency** – Overpower legitimate signals using spot, sweep, barrage, or smart jamming.
- **Maintain or Move the Jammer** – Keep the interference active or move it to a different frequency to avoid detection.

Did You Know? You can buy low-powered GPS jammers online for as little as $50 (though it's highly illegal in most countries).

5. Countering Jamming Attacks: How to Keep Satellites Talking

While jamming is frustratingly easy, stopping it is much harder. Here's how military, commercial, and security agencies fight back:

A. Frequency Hopping: The Classic "Dodge the Attack" Method

- Rapidly switching frequencies makes it harder for jammers to block signals.
- Used in military satellite communications and encrypted networks.

B. Directional Antennas: The "Ignore the Noise" Strategy

- Block interference by only accepting signals from expected satellite positions.
- Used in military, aviation, and high-security networks.

C. Anti-Jamming Software: AI to the Rescue

- Uses real-time signal analysis to detect and filter out jamming attempts.
- Some GNSS receivers now come with built-in anti-jamming features.

D. Power Boosting: Fight Noise with More Noise

- Increasing satellite signal strength helps overpower jammers.
- Not always possible, since satellites have limited power.

E. Alternative Navigation & Backup Systems

- Inertial Navigation Systems (INS): Can navigate without GPS.
- Fiber-Optic Communications: Less vulnerable than RF-based systems.

Who Uses These Defenses? The U.S. Air Force, NATO, and even commercial airlines use anti-jamming measures to protect against disruptions.

6. The Future of Satellite Jamming: Cyberwarfare & Beyond

As technology evolves, so do jamming techniques. Future threats include:

- **AI-Driven Jamming**: Hackers using machine learning to target specific devices.
- **Quantum-Resistant Communications**: Governments investing in quantum encryption to counter jamming.
- **Cyber-Physical Attacks**: Blending jamming with hacking to completely take over satellites.

The Bottom Line: The arms race between jammers and anti-jamming defenses is just getting started.

Conclusion: Because Nobody Likes a Silent Satellite

RF jamming isn't just an inconvenience—it's a major cybersecurity threat that can disrupt military operations, financial systems, and emergency communications. Whether it's nation-state cyberwarfare, GPS spoofing gangs, or just a rogue hacker with a radio transmitter, jamming is a real risk.

So, the next time your GPS mysteriously stops working, don't just assume it's bad weather—someone, somewhere, might just be playing the world's most annoying game of digital hide-and-seek.

6.2 Implementing Uplink and Downlink Jamming Attacks

Jamming Satellites: The Space Age Equivalent of Putting Gum in a Payphone

Ever wonder what it would be like to throw a giant "mute" button into space? Well, that's pretty much what uplink and downlink jamming attacks do. Imagine you're having an important phone call with someone on the other side of the world, and suddenly, someone hijacks the line and starts blasting static, alien conspiracy theories, or, worse—elevator music. That's uplink and downlink jamming in a nutshell, but with satellites and a whole lot more at stake.

In this section, we're going to take a deep dive into the mechanics of jamming, looking at both uplink and downlink attacks. We'll discuss how they're done, who's using them, and why they're a growing problem in space cybersecurity. By the end of this, you'll understand why governments are pouring billions into anti-jamming tech—and why the bad guys keep finding ways around it.

1. What's the Difference Between Uplink and Downlink Jamming?

Before we jump into the details, let's clarify what uplink and downlink mean in satellite communications:

☐ **Uplink** – This is when data is sent from Earth to a satellite (e.g., a command from a ground station to reposition a satellite).
☐ **Downlink** – This is when data is sent from the satellite back to Earth (e.g., GPS signals, TV broadcasts, or satellite internet).

So naturally, uplink jamming messes with the satellite's ability to receive signals, while downlink jamming disrupts the signals being sent back to Earth.

Uplink Jamming: Cutting Off the Satellite's Ears

If you can block a satellite from receiving legitimate signals, you can effectively silence it. This means:

📡 **Disrupting Military Communications** – Enemies can't send commands to military satellites.

🚀 **Blocking Navigation Updates** – GPS satellites won't receive correction data, making them unreliable.

🚀 **Hijacking Satellite Control** – If done right, uplink jamming can create a window for taking over a satellite.

Downlink Jamming: Making Satellites Talk Nonsense

This is about interfering with the signals coming from space, so the people on the ground get garbled or useless data. This can lead to:

🚀 **Disrupting GPS and Navigation Systems** – Planes, ships, and even your smartphone GPS can be misled.

🚀 **Jamming TV, Radio, and Internet Services** – Governments and hackers can block access to information.

🚀 **Messing with Military Intelligence** – Satellites can no longer relay surveillance footage or reconnaissance data.

2. How Are Uplink and Downlink Jamming Attacks Performed?

Alright, let's talk tactics. Performing these attacks requires specialized equipment, a solid understanding of radio frequencies, and questionable ethics (seriously, don't do this at home).

Step 1: Find the Right Frequency

Every satellite operates on a specific frequency band, such as:

📡 **L-Band (1-2 GHz):** Used for GPS and satellite phones.

📡 **C-Band (4-8 GHz):** Common for satellite TV and some military applications.

📡 **Ku & Ka-Bands (12-40 GHz):** Used for high-speed internet and communications.

To jam a satellite, you first need to identify what frequency it's using and what type of modulation it employs (AM, FM, digital signals, etc.).

Step 2: Generate the Jamming Signal

Once you know the target frequency, you need to blast it with interference using a radio transmitter and a high-gain antenna. The goal is to overpower the legitimate signal so that receivers can't distinguish it from the noise.

☐ Common Jamming Techniques:

✦ **Continuous Wave (CW) Jamming** – Constant, unmodulated noise to block a frequency.

✦ **Pulsed Jamming** – Bursts of interference at timed intervals.

✦ **Swept Jamming** – Rapidly scanning across frequencies to disrupt multiple signals.

Step 3: Maintain or Move the Jammer

Once the jamming signal is active, an attacker can either maintain it in one place or move it around to avoid detection. Many military and intelligence agencies use mobile jammers mounted on vehicles, aircraft, or even small drones.

💡 **Did You Know**? Some modern jammers use AI-based adaptive jamming, which automatically detects and disrupts active satellite signals in real time.

3. Who Uses Uplink and Downlink Jamming?

Jamming satellites isn't just something out of a James Bond movie—it happens all the time. Here are some of the biggest players:

Governments and Military Forces

🖋 **Electronic Warfare Units** – Used to disrupt enemy communications and reconnaissance.

🖋 **Censorship Operations** – Countries like North Korea and Iran have jammed satellite TV broadcasts to control information.

Cybercriminals and Hacktivists

🖋 **GPS Spoofing Gangs** – Used for hijacking shipments or fooling navigation systems.

🖋 **Rogue Hackers** – Have been known to jam satellites just for the thrill of it.

Corporations and Private Entities

🖋 **Corporate Espionage** – Some companies have allegedly used jamming to disrupt competitors' satellite networks.

🚀 **Pirate Broadcasters** – Illegal radio and TV stations sometimes jam signals to take over satellite channels.

4. Defending Against Uplink and Downlink Jamming

As jamming threats grow, the world is fighting back with new technologies. Here's how satellite operators and security experts are staying ahead of the game:

A. Frequency Hopping

🚀 Rapidly switching frequencies makes it harder for jammers to keep up.
🚀 Used by military and high-security communications networks.

B. Directional Antennas & Beamforming

🚀 These allow ground stations to filter out unwanted interference.
🚀 They focus signals toward legitimate satellites while ignoring jammers.

C. AI-Powered Anti-Jamming Algorithms

🚀 New AI-based software can detect jamming attempts in real-time.
🚀 Some systems can automatically switch to alternate frequencies.

D. Hardening Satellite Signals

🚀 Increasing transmission power can sometimes overpower a jammer.
🚀 New encryption techniques help prevent spoofing attacks alongside jamming.

E. Quantum Communications (The Future Solution?)

🚀 Quantum satellites could one day create signals that are impossible to jam.
🚀 Still in experimental phases, but could be a game-changer for space cybersecurity.

Conclusion: The Space Cyber Arms Race is Just Getting Started

Jamming satellites isn't just a hacker trick—it's a powerful cyberweapon used by governments, criminals, and rogue actors. From military conflicts to GPS fraud, uplink and downlink jamming can disrupt entire economies and defense systems.

The race between attackers and defenders is heating up, with AI-driven jamming, quantum encryption, and advanced anti-jamming measures leading the charge. But one thing's for sure—satellite security isn't just about launching metal into space anymore. It's about keeping those metal birds talking, listening, and NOT getting silenced by someone with a big enough antenna. 🚀😄

6.3 Distributed Denial-of-Service (DDoS) Attacks on Satellite Networks

Taking Satellites Down the "Internet Way" – DDoS in Space

Ever tried to get into your favorite coffee shop during a morning rush, only to find it so packed that you can't even squeeze through the door? That's pretty much how Distributed Denial-of-Service (DDoS) attacks work—except instead of caffeine-deprived hipsters, we're talking about malicious traffic flooding satellite networks until they can't function.

Now, you might be thinking, "Wait a minute, satellites are in SPACE! Can they even be DDoSed?" The short answer: Yes, and it's happening more than you think. Just because a satellite or its ground station is orbiting above us doesn't mean it's immune to one of the oldest tricks in the hacker playbook. In fact, satellite networks are particularly vulnerable because they rely on limited bandwidth and critical ground-based infrastructure to communicate with the world.

Let's break down how DDoS attacks on satellite networks work, who's doing them, and how we can fight back before the next space blackout.

1. How DDoS Attacks Work on Satellite Networks

Most people associate DDoS attacks with traditional internet services—taking down websites, gaming servers, or even government portals. But the same concept applies to satellite networks in two key ways:

A. Targeting Ground-Based Infrastructure

Satellites don't operate in isolation—they rely on ground stations, network gateways, and internet-connected infrastructure to function. If attackers flood these systems with junk traffic, they can disrupt:

🚀 **Satellite Internet Providers** – Think Starlink, Viasat, or Inmarsat getting knocked offline.

🚀 **Military Communications** – Secure defense satellites struggling to connect with command centers.

🚀 **Navigation Systems** – GPS data delivery failing, causing chaos for planes, ships, and even Uber drivers.

B. Overloading the Satellite's Own Links

Even though satellites are thousands of miles up, they still have limited bandwidth and processing power. Attackers can:

🚀 **Overload uplinks** – Flood the satellite with bogus requests, preventing legitimate users from getting through.

🚀 **Jam downlinks** – Send massive amounts of useless data to receivers on Earth, slowing down or crashing services.

The trick here? DDoS attacks on satellites aren't always brute force—they can be low-and-slow, slowly degrading service quality until entire systems become unusable.

2. Notable DDoS Attacks on Satellite Networks

If you think this is just a theory, think again. There have already been some major DDoS attacks targeting satellite services, with global consequences.

🚀 The Viasat Attack (2022)

◆ Just as Russian forces invaded Ukraine, a massive cyberattack hit Viasat's KA-SAT satellite network.

◆ Attackers disabled thousands of modems across Europe, cutting off satellite internet access.

◆ Ukrainian military communications and even wind turbines in Germany were affected.

🚀 GPS Jamming & DDoS in the South China Sea

◆ Maritime GPS disruptions have been linked to coordinated jamming and potential DDoS-style interference.

◆ Ships relying on satellite navigation reported GPS failures, causing confusion and security risks.

🚀 Satellite TV Disruptions in the Middle East

◆ Over the years, several Middle Eastern satellite networks have suffered DDoS-like service disruptions, suspected to be state-sponsored attacks to block broadcasts.

These attacks prove that DDoS threats aren't just about websites anymore—they're about controlling information, disrupting military operations, and even influencing wars.

3. How Attackers Perform DDoS on Satellites

DDoS attacks against satellites aren't that different from those against traditional networks. They typically involve:

A. Botnets & IoT Armies

◆ Attackers use networks of compromised IoT devices, routers, and even hacked satellite modems to launch large-scale attacks.
◆ Mirai-style botnets have already been caught targeting satellite networks.

B. Exploiting Open Services & Weak Security

◆ Many satellite-based ISPs and network providers still use poorly secured systems.
◆ Attackers use misconfigured DNS, NTP, or BGP services to amplify attacks.

C. Traffic Reflection & Amplification

◆ DDoS attackers spoof requests, bouncing them off unprotected servers to generate massive floods of traffic.
◆ A small attack request can trigger a 100x larger response, crippling the target.

D. Targeting VSAT Terminals & Satellite Modems

◆ Many satellite internet users rely on VSAT (Very Small Aperture Terminal) modems.
◆ Attackers can exploit vulnerabilities in these devices to launch localized DDoS floods.

4. Defense Strategies: How to Stop DDoS on Satellites

Stopping a DDoS attack is never easy, but securing satellite networks against these attacks is even harder. Still, there are several ways to mitigate and prevent large-scale disruptions:

A. AI-Powered Traffic Filtering

🚀 Machine learning-based DDoS detection can identify malicious traffic before it causes damage.
🚀 Space agencies and private companies are investing in real-time anomaly detection to spot DDoS traffic early.

B. Hardened Ground Stations & Network Infrastructure

🚀 Upgrading satellite internet modems and ground station networks to prevent hijacking.
🚀 Implementing stronger authentication and encryption to prevent unauthorized access.

C. Geo-Fencing & Signal Prioritization

🚀 Some modern satellites prioritize legitimate users over attack traffic.
🚀 Geo-fencing techniques help block malicious sources from accessing certain satellites.

D. Moving to Decentralized & Resilient Networks

🚀 Future satellite networks could use blockchain-based or decentralized protocols to distribute traffic and reduce single points of failure.
🚀 Companies like Starlink are experimenting with more resilient, self-healing networks.

E. Quantum Cryptography & Secure Satellite Links

🚀 Quantum encryption could make future satellite communications immune to traditional cyberattacks.
🚀 While still in experimental phases, it offers a potential long-term solution.

Conclusion: The Space DDoS Wars Are Just Beginning

It turns out, DDoS attacks aren't just an Earthly problem—they're very much a satellite problem too. With military, government, and commercial satellite networks increasingly relying on the internet, attackers will continue to exploit weak points to disrupt operations.

The good news? Space agencies, cybersecurity firms, and defense organizations are investing in new technologies to fight back. The bad news? The bad guys are getting smarter, faster, and more sophisticated.

One thing's for sure: the next big cyber war won't just be fought on Earth—it'll be fought in the stars. 🚀😆

6.4 Electromagnetic Interference (EMI) and Cyber-Physical Attacks

The Silent Killer of Satellite Signals—EMI and Cyber-Physical Mayhem

Picture this: You're on a road trip, belting out your favorite song when suddenly—static. Your radio signal is toast. Now imagine that happening to a satellite 35,000 km above Earth, but instead of just ruining a jam session, it knocks out communications for an entire region.

Welcome to the wild world of Electromagnetic Interference (EMI) and Cyber-Physical Attacks, where hackers, rogue states, and even accidental interference can turn space systems into giant paperweights. Whether it's deliberate jamming, accidental signal bleed, or full-scale cyber-physical warfare, satellites are more vulnerable than you think.

So, let's dive in—how can something as "simple" as interference mess with billion-dollar space infrastructure, and what can we do to stop it?

1. What Is Electromagnetic Interference (EMI)?

Electromagnetic Interference, or EMI, is any unwanted signal that disrupts normal communication. It comes in two flavors:

A. Natural EMI (Mother Nature's Unintentional Chaos)

Solar Flares & Cosmic Radiation – The Sun occasionally decides to throw a tantrum, sending waves of charged particles that disrupt radio and satellite signals.

Lightning & Geomagnetic Storms – Earth's atmosphere can sometimes mess with radio waves, causing temporary outages.

B. Artificial EMI (The "Oops" and the "Oh No" Types)

Unintentional EMI – Poorly shielded electronics (like an old microwave or a faulty power grid) can accidentally cause radio interference.

Intentional EMI (Jamming & Cyber-Physical Attacks) – Now we're talking deliberate attacks aimed at crippling satellite communications.

2. Types of Cyber-Physical Attacks on Satellites

A cyber-physical attack is where the digital and physical worlds collide, creating real-world consequences. While most cyberattacks happen in software, cyber-physical attacks target the actual hardware—satellites, ground stations, or the electromagnetic spectrum itself.

Here's how attackers can ruin a satellite operator's day:

A. Jamming (The Classic Sabotage Move)

Attackers blast a stronger signal on the same frequency as the satellite, effectively drowning out the real signal.

Military-grade jamming is used to disrupt GPS, military communications, and satellite TV.

In 2019, Iran allegedly jammed GPS signals, causing navigation failures for ships in the Persian Gulf.

B. Spoofing (The Ultimate Fake News for Satellites)

Attackers send false data to trick satellites or ground stations.

GPS spoofing has been used to redirect ships, aircraft, and even military drones.

In 2016, Russian GPS spoofing misled 20+ ships in the Black Sea, making their navigation systems believe they were miles inland.

C. High-Power Microwave (HPM) Attacks (Frying Circuits Like a Pro)

Special microwave weapons can overload satellite circuits, permanently damaging them.

In theory, an attacker could disable an entire satellite constellation by targeting ground stations.

D. Electromagnetic Pulses (EMP) (The Nuclear Option)

A nuclear detonation in space could generate a massive EMP, instantly frying multiple satellites.

The 1962 Starfish Prime test proved that one nuclear explosion could disable satellites thousands of kilometers away.

3. Real-World EMI & Cyber-Physical Incidents

These aren't just sci-fi scenarios—they've already happened:

🚀 2007 – GPS Jamming in North Korea

North Korea has repeatedly jammed GPS signals, disrupting airline navigation and military systems.

🚀 2011 – Alleged Hacking of U.S. Satellites

Reports surfaced that Chinese hackers gained access to U.S. Earth observation satellites via compromised ground stations.

🚀 2019 – Iran's Alleged GPS Spoofing

Ships in the Strait of Hormuz reported their GPS signals placing them in fake locations.

🚀 2022 – Russia's Cyber-Attack on Viasat

Just before the Ukraine invasion, Russian hackers crippled Viasat's KA-SAT network, disrupting military and civilian communications.

The message is clear: EMI and cyber-physical attacks are real threats, and they're happening right now.

4. Defending Satellites from EMI and Cyber-Physical Attacks

Now for the good news: We can fight back. Here's how:

A. Frequency Hopping & Spread Spectrum

🚀 Rapidly changing frequencies makes jamming much harder.
🚀 Military satellites use spread-spectrum techniques to avoid interference.

B. AI-Powered Signal Analysis

🚀 AI can detect jamming attempts in real-time and adjust transmission methods.
🚀 Some companies are working on AI-driven anomaly detection to prevent GPS spoofing.

C. Hardening Satellite Electronics

🚀 Satellites can be shielded against EMPs and microwave attacks.
🚀 Military-grade satellites already include radiation-hardened circuits.

D. Quantum Communications (The Future-Proof Solution?)

🚀 Quantum encryption makes satellite data nearly impossible to intercept or spoof.
🚀 China already launched quantum-secured satellites, paving the way for a new era of tamper-proof communications.

Conclusion: The Battle for the Electromagnetic Spectrum

EMI and cyber-physical attacks aren't just annoying signal disruptions—they're strategic weapons. From GPS jamming to EMP strikes, these attacks have the power to disrupt economies, mislead military forces, and even trigger conflicts.

As we become more dependent on space-based technology, the threats will only grow. But don't panic just yet—scientists, engineers, and security experts are working on next-gen defenses to keep our satellites (and our Wi-Fi) safe.

One thing's for sure: The future of space security isn't just about firewalls and encryption—it's about defending the very signals that keep our world connected. 🚀🔥

6.5 Countering Jamming and DoS Attacks in Space IoT Systems

Survival of the Fittest: How to Keep Satellites from Getting Bullied

Imagine you're trying to have an important phone call, but some prankster keeps shouting nonsense into your ear. That's basically what happens when a satellite gets jammed or hit with a Denial-of-Service (DoS) attack—except instead of just missing a call, you could be losing GPS navigation, global communications, or even national security data. Not ideal.

The reality is that satellites are prime targets for jamming and cyberattacks. Governments, hackers, and even overenthusiastic hobbyists have been disrupting satellite signals for years, sometimes for mischief, sometimes for war. But don't worry—we've got countermeasures, and I'm here to walk you through them.

1. How Jamming and DoS Attacks Disrupt Space IoT

Before we talk defenses, let's do a quick refresher on the main attack types:

A. Jamming: The Bullhorn of Disruption

Jamming works by overwhelming a signal with noise so that the real transmission is lost.

Uplink Jamming: Attackers flood the satellite's receiver with a stronger signal, preventing it from getting commands from the ground.

Downlink Jamming: Attackers block signals from the satellite to Earth, causing service outages for users.

🖊 **Example**: In 2011, Iran allegedly jammed U.S. military drones, forcing them to crash.

B. Denial-of-Service (DoS) Attacks: The Digital Flood

A DoS attack targets satellite ground stations or cloud-based infrastructure, overloading systems with excessive requests until they crash.

Distributed DoS (DDoS): Multiple sources flood satellite networks, causing massive delays or outages.

Protocol Exploitation: Attackers abuse vulnerabilities in satellite communication protocols to disrupt operations.

🚀 **Example**: The 2022 Russian cyberattack on Viasat's KA-SAT network disrupted Ukraine's military and civilian communications before the invasion.

2. Countermeasures: Fighting Back Against Jamming and DoS Attacks

Now, let's get to the good stuff—how to fight back.

A. Frequency Hopping: The Digital Shell Game

One of the best defenses against jamming is not staying in one place.

Satellites can switch frequencies rapidly, making it harder for attackers to jam the signal.

Military satellites already use spread spectrum techniques, like Direct Sequence Spread Spectrum (DSSS) and Frequency Hopping Spread Spectrum (FHSS), to avoid interference.

🚀 Think of it like dodging punches in a fight—if you keep moving, it's harder to get hit.

B. Adaptive Power Control: Outshining the Interference

If jamming is detected, satellites can automatically increase their signal power to overpower the interference.

This is called Adaptive Power Control (APC) and works best when paired with directional antennas that focus energy toward the intended receiver.

🚀 Imagine trying to talk over a loud crowd—so you just yell louder until they shut up.

C. AI-Driven Anomaly Detection: Smart Satellites Fight Back

AI and machine learning can detect unusual signal patterns and respond in real time.

Some satellites are now equipped with AI-powered countermeasures that identify and block suspicious signals before they cause harm.

🚀 Think of it as a satellite with built-in reflexes—it dodges attacks before they land.

D. Quantum Communications: The Future of Secure Satellite Links

Quantum encryption is basically cheating when it comes to security.

If someone tries to eavesdrop on a quantum-encrypted signal, the act of observing automatically changes the data, alerting the system.

China's Micius satellite was the first to successfully use quantum key distribution (QKD), proving that tamper-proof space communication is possible.

🚀 It's like setting up an alarm that goes off the moment a hacker even looks at your data.

E. Ground Station Hardening: Because Hackers Love Easy Targets

Many satellite attacks don't target the satellite itself—they go after ground stations and cloud networks.

Stronger firewalls, intrusion detection systems (IDS), and encrypted command channels make it harder for attackers to take over a satellite remotely.

🚀 Because what's the point of building a space fortress if you leave the front door open?

3. Case Studies: Real-World Countermeasures in Action

☐ NATO's Anti-Jamming Satellite Systems

NATO's Protected Tactical Waveform (PTW) allows secure military communications by resisting jamming attacks. It's already being used in modern SATCOM systems.

☐ Starlink's Rapid Response to Russian Jamming

When Russia tried to jam Starlink's satellite internet in Ukraine, SpaceX engineers patched the system in less than a day, proving that agile countermeasures work.

☐ The U.S. Air Force's Quantum Communications Experiment

The Air Force is testing quantum-secured satellite communications, aiming for hacker-proof military comms by 2030.

4. The Future of Satellite Defense: What's Next?

The space battlefield is evolving, and defense strategies need to keep up. Here's what the future holds:

◆ **AI-Driven Attack Prevention** – Satellites will autonomously detect and neutralize jamming attempts.

◆ **Laser-Based Communications** – Optical lasers can transmit data without radio frequencies, making jamming nearly impossible.

◆ **Decentralized Space IoT Networks** – Instead of relying on single satellites, future systems will use interconnected swarms that reroute around attacks.

The race between attackers and defenders isn't slowing down. But one thing's for sure: the future of satellite security is going to be one hell of a battle.

Final Thoughts: Stay Sharp, Stay Secure

If you've made it this far, congratulations—you now know how to fight satellite jamming and cyberattacks like a pro. But this is just the beginning. As hackers get smarter, so must our defenses.

Because let's face it—no one wants to wake up one day and find out their GPS thinks they're in the middle of the ocean or that their internet has mysteriously vanished.

Space isn't just for astronauts anymore—it's the next cyber battleground. And trust me, it's gonna be one hell of a fight. 🚀💥

Chapter 7: Hacking Satellite Ground Stations and IoT Infrastructure

If hacking an actual satellite sounds a little too ambitious, don't worry—sometimes, you don't have to go to space to break space systems. Why hijack a satellite in orbit when you can just exploit the ground station that controls it? Ground stations are often the weakest link in satellite security, and with enough skill, you can turn them into your personal space command center.

This chapter covers the architecture of satellite ground stations and their vulnerabilities, from outdated firmware to insecure cloud-based control platforms. We'll analyze common attack vectors, including IoT gateway exploits, unauthorized command injection, and software vulnerabilities, while also discussing best practices for securing satellite infrastructure against cyber threats.

7.1 Understanding Satellite Ground Station Architectures

Ground Stations: The Unsung Heroes of Space Communications

Let's be real—satellites get all the glory. They're up there floating in space, beaming signals down to Earth, looking all futuristic. But here's the thing: without ground stations, satellites are just expensive space junk. They need a way to talk to us, get instructions, and send back all the cool data they collect.

Think of it like this—your smartphone is only useful if it can connect to cell towers and Wi-Fi. Satellites work the same way. Their version of "cell towers" are ground stations, and these facilities are what keep space-based technology actually functional. Without them? Well, let's just say your GPS would send you straight into a lake, satellite TV would turn into static, and weather forecasts would be about as accurate as throwing darts at a calendar.

Now, if you're thinking "Great, ground stations are important, but how do they actually work?", then buckle up! We're about to break down the anatomy of a satellite ground station—from giant dish antennas to mission control centers.

1. The Core Components of a Ground Station

A satellite ground station is essentially the nerve center for managing satellite operations. It consists of several critical components, each playing a crucial role in communication, control, and security.

A. The Antenna System: The Big Ear of the Operation

The antenna system is the most recognizable part of any ground station—it's that giant dish that points toward the sky, listening for signals from space.

Parabolic Dishes – Large, high-gain antennas designed to receive weak signals from satellites thousands of kilometers away.

Phased Array Antennas – Modern stations use electronically steered antennas that don't need to physically move to track satellites.

Omnidirectional Antennas – Used for low-Earth orbit (LEO) satellites that pass overhead frequently.

🚀 **Fun fact**: The largest ground station antenna ever built was NASA's Deep Space Network (DSN) dish, measuring 70 meters (230 feet) wide!

B. The Tracking System: Keeping Satellites in Sight

Satellites don't just stay in one place (unless they're in geostationary orbit). Most satellites move across the sky, meaning ground stations need precise tracking systems to stay locked onto them.

Two-Line Element (TLE) Data – This is how ground stations calculate satellite orbits in real-time.

Autotracking Systems – Software that continuously adjusts the antenna to follow a satellite's movement.

Predictive Tracking – Uses orbital mechanics to anticipate where a satellite will be next.

🚀 Think of it like playing catch with someone running across a field—you have to predict where to throw the ball next!

C. The Telemetry, Tracking, and Command (TT&C) System

TT&C is the brains of the operation—it's responsible for:

Telemetry – Receiving health/status data from the satellite.

Tracking – Determining the satellite's exact location.

Commanding – Sending instructions to adjust satellite behavior.

Without TT&C, we wouldn't know if a satellite was working properly or even where it is in space. Imagine trying to drive a car blindfolded—that's what operating a satellite without TT&C would be like.

D. The Mission Control Center: The Decision-Making Hub

This is where human operators monitor satellite performance, analyze data, and make mission-critical decisions.

Satellite Engineers check system health.

Operators schedule communication windows.

Cybersecurity Teams protect against hacking and signal jamming.

🚀 Yes, people really do try to hack satellites! (We'll get into that later in the book.)

2. Types of Satellite Ground Stations

Not all ground stations are the same. They can be classified based on their mission, capabilities, and level of control over the satellite.

A. Mission Control Centers (MCCs)

Handle full control of satellites, including software updates and maneuvering.

Used by space agencies (NASA, ESA, ISRO, Roscosmos, etc.) and military organizations.

Often operate multiple satellites at once.

🚀 **Example**: NASA's Jet Propulsion Laboratory (JPL) manages deep-space missions like the Mars rovers.

B. Telemetry Stations

Focus on receiving data from satellites.

Often used for weather satellites, Earth observation, and scientific missions.

Typically don't send commands—they just collect information.

🚀 **Example**: NOAA operates telemetry stations for GOES weather satellites.

C. Tracking Stations

Specialized in precise location tracking of satellites.

Used for GPS, navigation satellites, and deep-space missions.

Work closely with astronomical observatories.

🚀 **Example**: The U.S. Space Force operates tracking stations for GPS satellites.

D. Commercial and Private Ground Stations

Owned by private companies for satellite internet, TV, and IoT communications.

Companies like SpaceX (Starlink), Amazon (Project Kuiper), and OneWeb operate their own networks.

Increasingly used for cloud-based satellite operations.

🚀 **Example**: SpaceX's Starlink network uses a global array of automated ground stations.

3. Security Challenges in Ground Stations

Now that we understand how ground stations work, let's talk about something every hacker loves: vulnerabilities. Ground stations are prime targets for cyberattacks, and here's why:

A. Hacking Ground Station Networks

Many older stations still use outdated software.

Poorly secured command links could allow unauthorized control of satellites.

Example: In 2008, hackers allegedly took control of two U.S. satellites through compromised ground stations.

B. Jamming and Signal Interference

Ground stations rely on clear frequencies to communicate with satellites.

Jammers can flood the signal with noise, disrupting operations.

Example: China and Russia have been accused of using jamming technology against military satellites.

C. Insider Threats and Social Engineering

Sometimes, the easiest way to hack a ground station is to trick an employee.

Example: In 2019, a hacker gained access to a satellite company's network by posing as an IT technician.

4. Future of Satellite Ground Stations

With increasing reliance on satellites, ground stations are evolving to be smarter, faster, and more secure.

A. AI-Powered Ground Stations

AI will automate tracking and security monitoring, reducing human error.

Example: Machine learning is being tested for real-time cyber threat detection.

B. Cloud-Based Satellite Control

Companies like Amazon Web Services (AWS) now offer cloud-based ground station services.

This allows for faster data processing but also introduces new cybersecurity risks.

C. Decentralized Ground Station Networks

Future satellites may communicate with multiple smaller ground stations, reducing single points of failure.

🚀 **The bottom line?** Ground stations may not be as flashy as the satellites they serve, but without them, space tech would be completely useless. Whether you're securing a military satellite or just binge-watching Netflix via Starlink, these stations are the true backbone of the space IoT revolution.

And now that you know how they work, let's talk about how hackers try to break in... 🛰️🛰️💻😼

7.2 Exploiting Vulnerabilities in Ground Station Software and Firmware

Ground Stations: The Big, Hackable Gateways to Space

Alright, let's be honest—when people think of hacking satellites, they imagine some Hollywood-level cyber-espionage, where an elite hacker wearing a hoodie takes control of a space station from their dimly lit basement. The reality? It's often way easier than that.

Why? Because satellites are managed from ground stations, and many of these facilities run outdated software, weakly encrypted communication protocols, and unsecured firmware. If a hacker gains control of a ground station, they can tamper with satellite commands, intercept sensitive data, or even hijack an entire satellite. Suddenly, that hoodie-wearing hacker scenario doesn't seem so far-fetched.

In this chapter, we'll break down the key vulnerabilities in ground station software and firmware, explain how hackers exploit them, and (for all the ethical hackers out there) discuss how to defend against these attacks.

1. Why Ground Stations Are Vulnerable to Cyberattacks

Ground stations may look high-tech, but many of them still run on legacy systems, and that's where the problems begin. Here's why:

A. Outdated Software and Operating Systems

Many ground stations still use old operating systems like Windows XP, outdated Linux distros, or even custom-built OS versions that haven't been updated in years.

These old systems have known vulnerabilities that attackers can exploit with publicly available exploits.

Example: In 2008, hackers gained control of two U.S. satellites by exploiting vulnerabilities in an outdated ground station network.

B. Weak Authentication and Access Control

Many ground station control systems lack multi-factor authentication (MFA).

Default credentials and hardcoded passwords are still common in some legacy software.

Some stations still use telnet (yes, telnet!) instead of encrypted SSH for remote access.

🚀 **Fun fact**: A 2020 security audit found NASA systems still using "1234" as a password on mission-critical systems. Let that sink in.

C. Vulnerabilities in Firmware and Embedded Systems

Ground stations rely on firmware-controlled hardware for antenna tracking, data processing, and radio frequency (RF) communication.

Many firmware components aren't digitally signed, meaning attackers can modify or inject malicious firmware updates.

Example: In 2019, a security researcher demonstrated a firmware backdoor in a commercial satellite modem that could be used to eavesdrop on data.

D. Unpatched Network Services and Protocols

Many ground stations use SNMP (Simple Network Management Protocol) and FTP (File Transfer Protocol) without proper security configurations.

Hackers can exploit buffer overflow vulnerabilities in these services to gain access to ground station networks.

Example: In 2021, researchers found multiple unpatched vulnerabilities in satellite ground equipment that could allow attackers to disrupt satellite communications.

2. How Hackers Exploit Ground Station Vulnerabilities

Now that we know why ground stations are vulnerable, let's talk about how attackers actually exploit these weaknesses.

A. Reverse Engineering Firmware

Attackers can extract firmware from ground station devices (like satellite modems, antennas, and data processing units).

They analyze the code to find backdoors, weak encryption, or unprotected command functions.

Once they identify vulnerabilities, they can modify the firmware and inject malicious code.

🚀 **Example Attack**: In 2018, researchers found that some satellite communication devices used in maritime and military operations had hardcoded backdoor credentials inside their firmware.

B. Exploiting Remote Access Weaknesses

Many ground stations allow remote access for maintenance, but some still use default credentials and insecure remote desktop protocols (RDP, VNC, and Telnet).

Hackers scan for open ports on the internet using tools like Shodan and Censys to find exposed systems.

Once they gain access, they can modify satellite commands, disrupt signals, or even spoof telemetry data.

🚀 **Real-World Example**: In 2014, a security researcher found exposed VNC connections on commercial satellite ground station software. If exploited, attackers could have taken full control of satellite operations.

C. Man-in-the-Middle (MITM) Attacks on Ground Station Networks

Many ground stations don't encrypt telemetry and command data properly, making them vulnerable to MITM attacks.

Hackers can intercept commands sent to satellites, alter them, or replay them to manipulate satellite behavior.

Tools like Software-Defined Radios (SDR) can be used to capture and analyze satellite communication signals.

🔏 **Example Attack**: In 2022, researchers demonstrated a MITM attack on a commercial satellite network, where they altered GPS signals to mislead tracking systems.

3. Securing Ground Station Software and Firmware

Now that we've covered how ground stations get hacked, let's discuss how to prevent it.

A. Implement Strong Authentication and Access Controls

Enforce multi-factor authentication (MFA) for all remote access systems.

Use role-based access control (RBAC) to limit who can modify critical systems.

Disable default credentials and use strong password policies.

B. Regular Software and Firmware Updates

Keep operating systems, software, and firmware updated with the latest security patches.

Implement automated patch management for ground station infrastructure.

Ensure that firmware updates are digitally signed and verified before installation.

C. Encrypt All Satellite Command and Control Links

Use end-to-end encryption for telemetry, tracking, and command (TT&C) communications.

Replace outdated encryption protocols (like DES or RC4) with AES-256 or quantum-resistant cryptography.

D. Secure Network Communications and Remote Access

Disable unnecessary network services like Telnet, FTP, and SNMP.

Use firewalls and intrusion detection systems (IDS) to monitor traffic.

Implement Zero Trust Architecture (ZTA) to prevent unauthorized access.

E. Conduct Regular Security Audits and Penetration Testing

Perform routine vulnerability assessments on ground station networks.

Use penetration testing tools to simulate real-world attacks.

Implement bug bounty programs to identify vulnerabilities before attackers do.

4. The Future of Ground Station Security

The cyber threats facing ground stations are only going to get worse as satellites become more integrated with AI, cloud computing, and IoT networks. Here's what's coming next:

A. AI-Driven Cyber Defense

AI-based threat detection will monitor real-time traffic and detect anomalies.

Machine learning algorithms will predict potential vulnerabilities before they're exploited.

B. Quantum Cryptography for Secure Satellite Communications

Future ground stations will adopt quantum-resistant encryption to prevent intercepted signals from being decrypted.

Quantum Key Distribution (QKD) will ensure secure satellite-to-ground station links.

C. Blockchain for Secure Satellite Command Authentication

Blockchain technology could be used to verify satellite command authenticity, preventing spoofing attacks.

Every command sent to a satellite would require cryptographic validation on a decentralized ledger.

Final Thoughts: Hack the Ground, Control the Skies

If you take away one thing from this chapter, let it be this: hackers don't need to touch a satellite to take control of it—they just need to exploit the ground station software and firmware.

Whether you're a cybersecurity researcher, penetration tester, or just a space nerd, understanding these vulnerabilities is crucial to securing modern space infrastructure. Because the last thing we need is some hacker turning a weather satellite into an orbital meme generator.

Now, let's move on to hijacking satellite IoT gateways—because things are about to get even crazier. 🚀💀

7.3 Hijacking Satellite IoT Gateways and Data Processing Centers

Welcome to the Gateway... of Chaos

If you've made it this far, congratulations! You've already learned how hackers exploit ground station vulnerabilities, so now let's take things up a notch—hijacking satellite IoT gateways and data processing centers.

Think of satellite IoT gateways as the middlemen between satellites and Earth-based networks. They handle all the data traffic, processing telemetry, and ensuring satellites communicate properly with ground infrastructure. In short, they're the brainstem of satellite operations—and that makes them a juicy target for hackers.

Now, if you're picturing some sci-fi-style hacking where a rogue hacker redirects satellites to beam cat videos to Mars, you're not entirely wrong. But in reality, hijacking an IoT gateway could lead to something even more dangerous—such as tampering with satellite navigation, disrupting military communications, or even manipulating weather data for economic or political gain.

In this chapter, we'll explore how attackers compromise satellite IoT gateways and data centers, the techniques they use, and (for those of you who don't want to end up in an Interpol investigation) how to secure these critical infrastructures.

1. What Are Satellite IoT Gateways and Data Processing Centers?

Before we get into hacking, let's first understand what these systems do.

A. Satellite IoT Gateways

Satellite IoT gateways are relay points that bridge the communication gap between:

Satellites and ground stations

Satellites and cloud-based data centers

Satellites and end-user IoT devices (e.g., maritime systems, oil rigs, aircraft, remote sensors)

These gateways collect, process, and transmit data from satellites, making them essential for:

Space-based IoT applications (e.g., GPS, environmental monitoring, defense systems)

Remote sensing and telemetry (e.g., disaster response, energy sector operations)

Commercial and industrial applications (e.g., aviation, agriculture, maritime navigation)

B. Data Processing Centers

Once a satellite transmits data to an IoT gateway, it's processed in data centers—which can be:

On-premise at ground stations

Cloud-based (e.g., AWS Ground Station, Microsoft Azure Orbital)

Hybrid systems (mix of private and public infrastructure)

These centers handle data storage, analytics, encryption, and command execution—making them another prime target for hackers.

2. How Hackers Hijack Satellite IoT Gateways

Now, let's get into the fun part—how cybercriminals can hijack these critical systems.

A. Exploiting Weak Authentication and Default Credentials

Many satellite IoT gateways still use factory-default credentials (think "admin/admin" or "password123").

Attackers scan for exposed IoT gateway interfaces using tools like Shodan and Censys.

Once they gain access, they can modify configurations, inject malicious firmware, or exfiltrate sensitive data.

🔍 **Real-World Example**: In 2021, security researchers found hundreds of exposed satellite IoT devices online with default credentials, making them easy targets for takeover.

B. Remote Code Execution (RCE) Attacks on Gateway Firmware

IoT gateways often run custom firmware with unpatched vulnerabilities.

Attackers use buffer overflow exploits and command injection attacks to execute malicious code remotely.

Once inside, they can disable encryption, reroute traffic, or even use the gateway as a botnet.

🔍 **Example Attack**: A well-known IoT worm, Mirai, has been modified to infect satellite IoT gateways—turning them into DDoS botnets.

C. Intercepting and Tampering with Satellite IoT Data

Many satellite IoT systems use unencrypted or weakly encrypted data transmissions.

Attackers can perform Man-in-the-Middle (MITM) attacks, intercepting and modifying:

Navigation data (e.g., altering GPS coordinates for ships or planes)

Environmental telemetry (e.g., falsifying weather reports to manipulate markets)

Military intelligence (e.g., spoofing reconnaissance data)

🚀 **Example Attack**: In 2018, hackers were able to intercept and modify weather satellite data, which could have been used to manipulate agriculture markets or disaster response efforts.

D. Cloud-Based Satellite IoT Takeovers

Many satellite data centers rely on cloud infrastructure (AWS, Azure, Google Cloud).

Attackers target misconfigured cloud storage buckets and API endpoints.

Once inside, they can exfiltrate terabytes of sensitive data or plant ransomware.

🚀 **Example**: In 2020, a security audit found that major satellite service providers had misconfigured AWS S3 buckets, exposing customer data, satellite logs, and even command files.

3. Securing Satellite IoT Gateways and Data Processing Centers

Now that we know how hackers exploit satellite IoT gateways, let's talk about how to defend them.

A. Enforce Strong Authentication and Access Controls

Disable default credentials and require unique, complex passwords.

Implement multi-factor authentication (MFA) for all remote access points.

Use Zero Trust Architecture (ZTA) to ensure strict access control.

B. Secure Firmware and Software Updates

Require digitally signed firmware updates to prevent tampering.

Regularly patch known vulnerabilities in IoT gateway firmware.

Enable automatic security updates for satellite-linked cloud services.

C. Encrypt Data Transmissions End-to-End

Implement AES-256 encryption for telemetry, command, and IoT data transmissions.

Use post-quantum cryptographic methods to future-proof encryption.

Prevent MITM attacks with VPN tunneling and network segmentation.

D. Monitor and Audit IoT Gateways for Anomalies

Deploy AI-driven intrusion detection systems (IDS) to flag suspicious activity.

Conduct regular penetration testing to identify vulnerabilities before attackers do.

Enable real-time logging and alerts to detect unauthorized access.

E. Secure Cloud-Based Satellite Data Centers

Configure cloud storage with proper access controls (no open S3 buckets!).

Restrict API access to trusted sources only.

Use blockchain-based authentication for secure satellite command execution.

4. The Future of Securing Satellite IoT

As satellite IoT expands, security risks will only increase. Future solutions will include:

AI-powered autonomous cybersecurity, capable of detecting and stopping attacks in real time.

Quantum encryption for ultra-secure satellite links, preventing future decryption threats.

Decentralized authentication using blockchain, ensuring satellite commands cannot be tampered with.

With more 5G and space-based IoT networks on the horizon, satellite security must evolve—or else we'll be dealing with an entire industry of space-based cybercrime.

Final Thoughts: Hack the Gateway, Hack the Satellite

If you control the IoT gateway, you control the data. And if you control the data, you control the satellite network. Hackers know this, and so should you.

So whether you're an ethical hacker, security researcher, or just a space geek, securing satellite IoT gateways is one of the most critical challenges in modern cybersecurity.

Now, let's move on to attacking cloud-based satellite control platforms—because what's better than hacking satellites? Hacking their cloud servers. 🚀💀

7.4 Attacking Cloud-Based Satellite Control Platforms

Welcome to the Cloud… of Doom ☁️ 💀

Ah, the cloud—where all our problems magically disappear, right? Wrong.

In the satellite world, cloud-based control platforms have revolutionized how we manage, command, and monitor satellites. Companies like AWS Ground Station, Microsoft Azure Orbital, and Google Cloud's satellite solutions allow organizations to control satellites without needing to build expensive ground stations. Sounds great, right?

Well, guess what? Hackers love the cloud too. Why spend millions on radio gear and SDRs when you can just phish an admin's AWS credentials and take over a satellite from your couch?

In this chapter, we'll explore how attackers compromise cloud-based satellite platforms, exploit misconfigurations, and hijack entire satellite networks—and, of course, how to prevent it (unless you enjoy the thought of rogue satellites causing chaos).

1. Why Satellites are Moving to the Cloud

Before we talk hacking, let's break down why satellites are increasingly cloud-dependent.

A. Cost Efficiency

Traditional satellite ground stations cost millions to build and maintain.

Cloud-based platforms eliminate the need for dedicated hardware.

B. Scalability and Global Access

Companies can control multiple satellites from anywhere via a web dashboard.

Cloud platforms allow for fast deployments and global data distribution.

C. Data Processing & AI Integration

Cloud platforms provide AI-driven analytics for satellite imagery, GPS, and telemetry.

This allows for faster decision-making and automated satellite operations.

D. Security (Ironically, Also a Weakness)

Cloud providers offer encryption, access controls, and threat detection.

But... as we'll see next, these systems are only as strong as their weakest link.

2. How Hackers Attack Cloud-Based Satellite Platforms

Let's get into the fun part—how hackers take over satellites via cloud attacks.

A. Credential Theft & Phishing

Hackers don't need to brute-force satellite signals when they can just steal login credentials.

Phishing attacks trick employees into revealing AWS/Azure credentials.

Credential stuffing (using leaked passwords) gives attackers cloud access.

Session hijacking lets hackers exploit logged-in users.

🚀 **Example**: In 2022, a major cloud provider reported that hackers breached customer cloud instances using stolen API keys—imagine if that customer controlled satellites.

B. Misconfigured Cloud Storage & APIs

Unprotected S3 buckets and open APIs expose satellite control files and telemetry data.

Hackers use tools like Shodan and Censys to find these exposed assets.

Once inside, attackers can modify command sequences, intercept satellite data, or even brick entire fleets.

🚀 **Real-World Example:** In 2020, security researchers found thousands of misconfigured cloud storage instances containing sensitive aerospace and satellite data.

C. Exploiting Cloud Compute Services

Attackers can launch cryptojacking malware on cloud-based satellite instances.

Denial-of-service (DoS) attacks can overwhelm cloud-based control systems.

Supply chain attacks (e.g., injecting malicious software updates) can compromise entire fleets of satellites.

🚀 **Case Study:** In 2021, North Korean hackers targeted cloud-based satellite services, attempting to deploy malware via compromised software updates.

D. Ransomware in Space

Hackers can encrypt satellite control files and demand ransom to restore access.

Attacks on cloud-based platforms can lock operators out of their own satellites.

Ransomware can target satellite imaging data, navigation systems, and even military comms.

🚀 **Example**: In 2022, a ransomware attack on a satellite internet provider disrupted thousands of European broadband connections.

3. Securing Cloud-Based Satellite Platforms

Okay, now that we've scared the hell out of you, let's talk about how to prevent these attacks.

A. Implement Zero Trust Security

No one should have automatic trust—even internal users must be verified.

Require multi-factor authentication (MFA) for all cloud admin accounts.

Use role-based access controls (RBAC) to limit permissions.

B. Secure APIs and Cloud Storage

Encrypt all data at rest and in transit (AES-256, TLS 1.3).

Restrict API access to known IPs and authenticated users.

Regularly scan for misconfigured cloud assets using security tools.

C. Monitor for Anomalies & Insider Threats

Deploy AI-powered threat detection to spot suspicious cloud activity.

Use log monitoring tools (e.g., AWS GuardDuty, Azure Sentinel) to flag unauthorized access.

Limit employee access—if someone doesn't need satellite control, don't let them have it.

D. Regular Security Audits & Penetration Testing

Conduct cloud penetration tests to find vulnerabilities before attackers do.

Use bug bounty programs to encourage ethical hacking research.

Audit all software dependencies and third-party services for backdoors.

4. The Future of Cloud-Based Satellite Security

As satellites become more dependent on cloud services, the attack surface will only grow. Upcoming security trends include:

✓ AI-driven threat detection to identify attacks in real time.

✓ Post-quantum encryption to secure satellite-cloud communications.

✓ Blockchain-based authentication for satellite commands.

✓ Decentralized cloud infrastructure to prevent single points of failure.

With more satellites connecting to cloud services, attackers will keep finding new ways to exploit them. Cybersecurity must evolve—or we risk losing control of the very satellites that power our world.

Final Thoughts: The Cloud is a Double-Edged Sword

Sure, the cloud is amazing—but hackers love it just as much as we do. If security isn't a top priority, satellites can be hijacked, locked down, or turned into expensive space debris.

So, the next time someone says, "It's fine, we use AWS for satellite control," remind them:

☞ *"Yeah, so do hackers."* 😼 🚀

7.5 Securing Ground Stations Against Cyber Intrusions

Ground Stations: The Cosmic ATM Machines for Hackers 🚀💰

Imagine if banks left their ATM networks completely unprotected, allowing hackers to walk up, press a few buttons, and drain every account. Now, replace "banks" with satellite ground stations, and you've got a pretty good idea of what's happening in space cybersecurity.

Ground stations are the brains behind satellite operations—they send commands, receive data, and control everything from navigation to military communications. Unfortunately, many ground stations run outdated software, use weak passwords, or are exposed to the internet. You don't need a billion-dollar hacking lab to exploit them—sometimes, a simple misconfigured firewall or a forgotten default admin password is enough.

In this chapter, we'll explore how hackers infiltrate ground stations, why these attacks are dangerous, and—most importantly—how we can secure these critical systems before satellites start taking orders from cybercriminals.

1. Why Ground Stations Are a Prime Target for Hackers

Ground stations serve as the command-and-control centers for satellites. If an attacker gains access to a ground station, they can:

Intercept or manipulate satellite communications (hello, espionage!).

Hijack satellites for ransom or malicious purposes.

Disrupt GPS, weather tracking, and military operations.

Inject false data or alter satellite imaging (imagine deepfake satellite imagery).

Completely decommission or "brick" a satellite, turning it into space junk.

Given how critical they are, you'd expect Fort Knox-level security, right? Not quite.

2. Common Attack Vectors on Ground Stations

Let's dive into the main ways hackers compromise ground stations.

A. Weak Authentication & Credential Attacks

Many ground stations still use default or weak passwords (like "admin123").

Phishing attacks trick engineers into giving away login credentials.

Credential stuffing (using leaked passwords from data breaches) gives hackers access.

🔏 **Example**: In 2022, security researchers found that some satellite control interfaces were accessible via the public internet—with default credentials still enabled.

B. Vulnerable Software & Unpatched Systems

Many ground stations run legacy software that hasn't been updated in years.

Exploitable vulnerabilities in SCADA, Linux servers, and custom satellite software.

Attackers can remotely execute malicious commands by exploiting these weaknesses.

🚀 **Example**: In 2018, the US government reported multiple cyber intrusions into satellite control networks, where attackers exploited unpatched systems.

C. Insider Threats & Physical Security Gaps

Disgruntled employees can plant backdoors or leak sensitive data.

Attackers can physically access ground stations by posing as contractors.

Many stations lack biometric authentication or multi-layered access controls.

🚀 **Example**: In 2017, a former engineer at a satellite firm leaked classified access credentials after being fired.

D. Network Attacks & Remote Exploits

Many ground stations have direct internet exposure (big mistake).

Attackers use Shodan, Censys, and Nmap to find open ports and vulnerabilities.

Man-in-the-middle (MITM) attacks allow hackers to alter command transmissions.

🚀 **Example**: Hackers have used MITM attacks to reroute and modify GPS data, leading to spoofed locations.

3. How to Secure Ground Stations from Cyber Intrusions

Now that we've covered how ground stations get hacked, let's talk about how to lock them down.

A. Implement Strong Authentication & Access Controls

✓ Multi-Factor Authentication (MFA): No single-password access.

✓ Role-Based Access Controls (RBAC): Engineers should only access what they need.

✅ Hardware Security Tokens: Use physical security keys for authentication.

✅ Zero Trust Security: Always verify, never assume trust.

B. Patch Software & Use Hardened Operating Systems

✅ Regularly update satellite control software to fix vulnerabilities.

✅ Use hardened Linux distros (e.g., Qubes OS, SELinux) for secure operations.

✅ Implement firmware security: No unsigned software updates!

C. Network Security & Intrusion Detection

✅ Segment ground station networks to prevent lateral movement.

✅ Deploy firewalls and VPNs to restrict access.

✅ Use IDS/IPS (Intrusion Detection/Prevention Systems) to flag anomalies.

🚀 **Pro Tip**: Use AI-driven anomaly detection to spot unusual login patterns and prevent unauthorized access.

D. Secure Physical Access & Prevent Insider Threats

✅ Implement biometric authentication (fingerprint, retina scans).

✅ Use video surveillance and restricted access zones.

✅ Regularly audit employee activity to catch potential insider threats.

🚀 **Case Study**: In 2019, an employee at a satellite company was caught trying to sell access credentials on the dark web—strict auditing exposed the breach.

4. Future-Proofing Ground Station Security

Cyber threats aren't going away, and as satellites become more autonomous, securing ground stations will be even more critical. The future of ground station security will likely include:

✅ AI-powered cyber defenses that detect and neutralize threats in real time.

✅ Quantum encryption for unbreakable communication security.

✅ Blockchain-based access controls to prevent unauthorized satellite commands.

✅ Air-gapped backup control systems in case of cyberattacks.

The reality is simple: ground stations are the gateway to space, and if we don't secure them, we might wake up one day to find our satellites hacked, hijacked, or held for ransom.

Final Thoughts: Lock It Down Before It's Too Late 🚀🔒

If hackers take over a ground station, they take over the satellites—and trust me, you don't want some cybercriminal in a basement ordering satellites to self-destruct or beam cat videos to the International Space Station.

So, next time someone asks "Why should we invest in ground station security?", tell them this:

☞ "Because controlling satellites should be harder than logging into Netflix." 😄

Chapter 8: Reverse Engineering and Exploiting Satellite Firmware

Reverse engineering firmware is like peeling back the layers of a mystery burrito—you never know what you're going to find. Hardcoded credentials? Weak encryption? Maybe even a debug mode that lets you bypass authentication? Satellites might be floating high above us, but their software is still vulnerable to the same kinds of attacks that plague Earth-bound IoT devices.

In this chapter, we'll explore techniques for extracting and analyzing satellite firmware, identifying security flaws, and exploiting hardcoded credentials. We'll also discuss reverse engineering proprietary communication protocols and injecting backdoors, while emphasizing best practices for developing secure satellite firmware.

8.1 Extracting and Analyzing Satellite Firmware and Software

Firmware: The Hidden Treasure Chest of Satellites 🗄️

Picture this: You've just found an old, dusty treasure chest in an abandoned space station (okay, maybe just in a ground station's server room). You know it's full of secrets, but it's locked—and the key is nowhere to be found. That, my friends, is what hacking satellite firmware feels like.

Firmware is the brains behind every satellite operation—from steering in orbit to encrypting communications. If you can extract and analyze it, you can uncover vulnerabilities, hardcoded credentials, and even hidden backdoors. But here's the catch: satellite firmware isn't meant to be tampered with—and manufacturers go to great lengths to keep it locked down.

In this section, we'll break into that metaphorical treasure chest, exploring the tools and techniques hackers (both ethical and not-so-ethical) use to extract, analyze, and sometimes even modify satellite firmware. Because, let's be honest—what's the point of hacking space tech if you can't have a little fun with it? 🚀

1. What is Satellite Firmware, and Why Does It Matter?

Satellite firmware is the low-level software that controls a satellite's hardware components. It tells the satellite how to communicate, execute commands, and protect itself. Here's why hackers love getting their hands on it:

Firmware can contain hardcoded credentials (factory passwords, SSH keys, and API tokens).

Security flaws in firmware can be exploited to hijack satellite functions.

Reverse-engineering firmware helps attackers find hidden backdoors or vulnerabilities.

Tampered firmware can lead to bricked satellites, intercepted communications, or complete takeovers.

2. Extracting Satellite Firmware: Getting Past the Security Layers

So, how do hackers actually get their hands on satellite firmware? Here are the top ways:

A. Dumping Firmware from Satellite Hardware

Some hackers gain access to satellite components through:

🔧 **JTAG & UART Interfaces** – Hardware debugging ports that provide direct access to firmware.
🔌 **SPI Flash Chips** – The memory storage that holds the firmware—can be dumped using a programmer.
▢▢ **Chip-Off Techniques** – Physically removing the flash chip and extracting its contents.

🚀 **Real-World Example**: Researchers have successfully extracted firmware from commercial satellite modems using JTAG debuggers, revealing default admin passwords and unpatched security flaws.

B. Extracting Firmware from Satellite Ground Station Systems

Sometimes, satellite firmware isn't even in space—it's sitting in update files, backups, or ground station software. Hackers often find firmware by:

💾 Searching firmware update files on ground station servers.
▢▢ Exploring cloud-based storage for unprotected firmware repositories.

🔓 Using Shodan/Censys to find exposed update servers.

🔎 **Case Study**: A satellite firmware update server was once left exposed to the internet, allowing researchers to download and analyze firmware images.

C. Downloading Publicly Available Firmware

Believe it or not, some manufacturers accidentally publish firmware updates online. Hackers can search for:

🔍 Firmware update packages on official support websites.
📁 Repositories on GitHub, FTP servers, or archived hacker forums.
⬜⬜ Leaked firmware dumps on underground cybercriminal markets.

🔎 **Pro Tip**: If you ever find yourself reverse-engineering firmware, always check the vendor's website first—you'd be surprised how often they leave the keys under the doormat.

3. Analyzing Extracted Firmware for Vulnerabilities

Once you've got your hands on satellite firmware, it's time to dig through it like a hacker archeologist. Here's how professionals analyze firmware:

A. Unpacking the Firmware Image

Firmware files are often compressed or encrypted. To start analyzing, hackers use:

📦 **Binwalk** – Scans firmware for file signatures, extracting compressed sections.
🔍 **Firmwalker** – Searches firmware for credentials, keys, and configs.
⬜⬜ **QEMU/Emulation** – Runs the firmware in a virtual environment for testing.

🔎 **Example**: Researchers used Binwalk to extract a satellite modem's firmware and found an unprotected SSH private key—a golden ticket for remote access.

B. Searching for Hardcoded Credentials and Secrets

Once extracted, hackers comb through the firmware for:

🔑 Hardcoded passwords (often found in config files).

🔐 API keys and encryption keys left by careless developers.

🔍 Debugging backdoors (hidden admin access points).

🚀 **Case Study**: In 2020, researchers found root-level hardcoded credentials in the firmware of a commercial satellite router—exposing thousands of systems to remote takeover.

C. Reverse Engineering Firmware Binaries

To understand how firmware operates, hackers decompile it using:

⚙️ **Ghidra or IDA Pro** – Decompiles firmware into readable assembly code.

📟 **Radare2** – A powerful open-source reverse-engineering tool.

☐☐ **Static and dynamic analysis** – Testing how firmware reacts to different inputs.

🚀 **Pro Tip**: Always look at error messages in firmware—they often reveal debugging info or secret admin functions.

4. Modifying & Injecting Backdoors into Firmware

Now, for the really fun part—modifying firmware. Hackers can:

Inject malicious code to gain persistent access.

Modify encryption routines to weaken security.

Change satellite configurations to reroute data.

🚀 **Example**: Ethical hackers once modified a satellite modem's firmware to create a backdoor that sent all traffic to their own servers—exposing a major security flaw.

5. How to Secure Satellite Firmware from Attacks

After seeing how easy it is to hack firmware, let's talk about how to defend against these attacks.

✅ **Use Firmware Encryption & Secure Boot** – Ensure firmware can't be modified or executed without verification.

✅ **Eliminate Hardcoded Credentials** – No more "admin/admin123" in firmware!

✅ **Implement Remote Firmware Integrity Checks** – Detect unauthorized modifications.

✅ **Regularly Update Firmware** – Patch vulnerabilities before hackers find them.

✅ **Use AI-Based Threat Detection** – Identify abnormal satellite behavior caused by hacked firmware.

Final Thoughts: Don't Let Satellites Become Space Zombies 🧟‍♂️

If firmware isn't secured, satellites become remote-controlled space zombies, obeying hackers instead of their rightful operators. And trust me, the last thing we need is a ransomware attack in orbit.

So, next time you hear someone say, "Nobody hacks satellite firmware," just smile and tell them:

☞ "That's exactly what they want you to think." ☺

8.2 Finding and Exploiting Hardcoded Credentials in Satellite Systems

Hardcoded Credentials: The Skeleton Key to Satellite Systems 🔑

Imagine this: You just bought a fancy new safe to store your most valuable secrets. It's state-of-the-art, reinforced with steel, and comes with an ultra-secure lock. But then, the manufacturer helpfully prints the default master code right on the manual—and worse, they use the same code for every single safe they sell.

Sounds ridiculous, right? Well, welcome to the world of hardcoded credentials in satellite systems—where manufacturers (even the biggest aerospace companies) sometimes bake in passwords, API keys, and SSH credentials right into the firmware, essentially leaving the front door wide open for attackers.

In this section, we'll uncover how hackers find and exploit these security lapses to gain unauthorized access to satellites and ground stations. Spoiler alert: It's often easier than you'd think.

1. What Are Hardcoded Credentials, and Why Are They a Problem?

Hardcoded credentials are passwords, API keys, or cryptographic secrets that are permanently written into firmware or software. Unlike user-configured credentials, they can't be changed easily—which means that if an attacker discovers them, every system using that firmware is at risk.

Here's why hardcoded credentials in satellite systems are a nightmare for security:

🚀 **They provide instant access** – Once found, they let attackers log in as privileged users.

🔒 **They're the same across multiple devices** – Meaning one leaked password could compromise an entire fleet of satellites.

🎯 **They're easy to find** – Hackers can extract them from firmware, logs, or even vendor documentation.

☐ **They're often overlooked** – Many satellite systems assume "security by obscurity" will keep them safe.

Real-world example? In 2018, security researchers found hardcoded SSH keys in the firmware of a commercial satellite modem—allowing anyone with the key to remotely access thousands of devices worldwide. Not great for cybersecurity.

2. How Hackers Find Hard Coded Credentials in Satellite Systems

Finding hard coded credentials is like a digital treasure hunt—except the treasure is a root password that unlocks satellite control systems. Here are some of the top techniques attackers use:

A. Extracting Credentials from Satellite Firmware

Hackers often start by dumping firmware from satellite equipment (e.g., ground station modems, satellite routers, or control software). Once they have the firmware file, they search for credentials using:

🔍 **Binwalk** – Extracts compressed files and finds readable text in firmware.
☐☐ **Strings Command** – Searches for plaintext credentials, API keys, and passwords.
🏛 **Ghidra / IDA Pro** – Decompiles firmware to analyze login functions and encryption keys.

🚀 **Example**: A hacker once extracted firmware from a satellite uplink device and found a root-level Telnet password buried in a configuration file. With that single password, they could log into every unit using that firmware.

B. Searching Configuration Files and Logs

Some of the easiest-to-find credentials are stored in plaintext within configuration files, logs, or environment variables. Hackers look for:

📁 **/etc/passwd and /etc/shadow files** – Contain user credentials in Unix-based systems.

🗝️ **Config files** – May store admin credentials or default passwords.

📑 **Debug logs** – Often include API keys or authentication tokens.

🚀 **Example**: A security researcher found default SSH keys stored in an update log file for a satellite control system, giving them full remote access.

C. Reverse Engineering Software Binaries

If credentials aren't stored in plaintext, hackers may reverse-engineer the software to extract them. They use tools like:

🔲 **Radare2** – Analyzes binaries for authentication functions.

🔍 **Ghidra / IDA Pro** – Looks for hardcoded password verification logic.

📑 **Dynamic Analysis** – Runs the firmware in an emulator to observe login behavior.

🚀 **Example**: Hackers once found a backdoor password in a commercial satellite router by analyzing its firmware with IDA Pro. The manufacturer had intentionally included the password for remote debugging—but forgot to remove it before production. Oops.

D. Searching the Internet for Leaked Credentials

Believe it or not, some hardcoded credentials can be found with a simple Google search. Hackers use:

🔎 **Shodan/Censys** – To find exposed satellite devices running default credentials.

📁 **GitHub Dorking** – To search for leaked API keys in public repositories.

🔲 **Pastebin & Dark Web Dumps** – To find stolen credentials from past breaches.

🚀 **Example**: In 2019, researchers found hardcoded admin credentials for a satellite ground station system publicly listed in an old user manual. It was literally in the PDF documentation.

3. Exploiting Hardcoded Credentials: How Hackers Use Them

Once attackers find hardcoded credentials, the real fun begins. Here's what they do next:

A. Gaining Remote Access

With hardcoded credentials, hackers can:

▢▢ Log into satellite modems, routers, and control systems using SSH, Telnet, or web admin panels.
🔒 Bypass authentication to execute privileged commands.
📡 Intercept and manipulate satellite data.

🚀 **Case Study**: A penetration test revealed that a major satellite ISP never changed default SSH passwords on customer terminals—allowing attackers to access thousands of devices remotely.

B. Moving Laterally to Other Systems

Once inside, attackers can:

🔑 Extract additional credentials (e.g., database passwords, encryption keys).
📡 Modify satellite configurations to redirect traffic or disable security features.
🎭 Impersonate legitimate users to gain deeper access.

🚀 **Example**: Hackers used hardcoded FTP credentials in a ground station system to pivot into mission control networks, accessing sensitive satellite telemetry data.

C. Planting Backdoors for Persistent Access

To maintain control, attackers can:

▢▢ Modify firmware to create persistent backdoors.
▢ Replace authentication mechanisms with their own credentials.
🔍 Disable security features to prevent detection.

🚀 **Case Study**: A hacker modified a satellite ground station's firmware to automatically accept a secret login—allowing them to regain access even if the system was reset.

4. How to Defend Against Hard Coded Credential Exploits

So, how do we stop hackers from using these tricks? Here are some best practices for securing satellite systems:

✅ **Remove Hardcoded Credentials** – Always use dynamically generated passwords instead.

✅ **Implement Two-Factor Authentication (2FA)** – Even if a password is leaked, 2FA prevents unauthorized access.

✅ **Use Secure Boot and Firmware Encryption** – Prevent attackers from extracting and modifying firmware.

✅ **Regularly Audit Firmware for Hard Coded Secrets** – Run automated scans to catch vulnerabilities.

✅ **Change Default Credentials Immediately** – Never use factory-default passwords in production systems.

Final Thoughts: Stop Leaving the Key Under the Doormat!

Hardcoded credentials are one of the dumbest security mistakes in the satellite industry—but they're still incredibly common. If we want to keep satellites secure, we need to stop leaving the keys to the kingdom inside the firmware.

Because if hackers can find them, you can bet that space pirates, rogue nations, and cybercriminals will too. And the last thing we need is a bunch of hackers taking over satellites for ransom or space trolling. 🚀😄

8.3 Reverse Engineering Proprietary Satellite Communication Protocols

Hacking Satellite Protocols: When Your Homework is Literally Rocket Science 🚀

Reverse engineering satellite communication protocols is a bit like trying to read an ancient alien language—except the aliens are aerospace engineers, and they definitely don't want you understanding their work.

Manufacturers design proprietary protocols to keep satellite communications secure, efficient, and (let's be honest) as confusing as possible for outsiders. Unlike standard networking protocols like HTTP or TCP/IP, these custom satellite protocols aren't well-documented, meaning that if you want to break in, you have to figure them out yourself.

And that's where the real fun begins. In this section, we'll dive into how hackers reverse-engineer these secretive protocols to decode signals, manipulate transmissions, and even hijack satellite commands. Buckle up—this is the deep end of satellite hacking.

1. What are Proprietary Satellite Communication Protocols?

Satellite systems don't just use one communication protocol—they use a stack of them, each with its own quirks and security risks. These protocols handle everything from sending telemetry data to relaying mission-critical commands.

Here's a breakdown of where proprietary protocols are used in satellite systems:

📡 **Uplink & Downlink Control**: The protocol that governs how the ground station communicates with the satellite and vice versa.
☐ **Payload Data Transmission**: The method satellites use to send data (images, sensor readings, etc.) back to Earth.
☐ **Error Correction & Compression**: Ensures signals survive the harsh environment of space.
🔐 **Encryption & Authentication Layers**: Protects data from unauthorized access—assuming it's implemented correctly (spoiler: it often isn't).

Since these protocols are often custom-built by manufacturers like SpaceX, Boeing, or Lockheed Martin, there's very little public documentation available. That's why attackers and researchers turn to reverse engineering.

2. How Hackers Reverse Engineer Satellite Protocols

Breaking open a proprietary protocol requires a mix of radio hacking, firmware analysis, and cryptanalysis. Here are the most common techniques used:

A. Signal Capture & Analysis

If you want to understand a satellite's communication protocol, step one is to listen in.

Hackers use Software-Defined Radios (SDRs) to capture signals from satellites and analyze them for patterns. Popular tools include:

☐ **HackRF / BladeRF / RTL-SDR** – Low-cost SDRs used to capture satellite signals.
🔍 **GQRX / SDR#** – Software to visualize and demodulate captured signals.
📶 **GNU Radio** – A powerful framework for signal processing and decoding.

🔦 **Example**: Researchers once used SDRs to decode Iridium satellite pager messages, proving that certain satellite networks were sending unencrypted data over the air.

B. Protocol Fuzzing & Packet Analysis

Once you've captured a transmission, the next step is breaking it down into its core components.

💼 **Wireshark** – Can analyze structured binary protocols if data is properly demodulated.
🔋 **Scapy** – Helps craft and send custom packets to test how a protocol responds.
☐☐ **Custom Python Scripts** – Often required to parse and manipulate raw satellite data.

🔦 **Example**: A security researcher discovered a vulnerability in DVB-S broadcast signals by fuzzing data packets and observing how the satellite responded to malformed transmissions.

C. Firmware Extraction & Reverse Engineering

Sometimes the easiest way to decode a protocol isn't by intercepting transmissions, but by ripping it straight from the source—the satellite's firmware or the ground station software.

🔧 **Binwalk** – Extracts compressed files and hidden firmware components.
☐☐ **Ghidra / IDA Pro** – Disassembles binaries to reveal authentication functions.
📖 **Static & Dynamic Analysis** – Runs the firmware in an emulator to observe protocol behavior.

🔦 **Example**: Hackers once dumped firmware from a satellite ground station modem and found a proprietary encryption algorithm hardcoded into the software, allowing them to decrypt previously captured transmissions.

D. Brute-Forcing & Cryptanalysis

Even if a satellite protocol is encrypted, there's always a chance the encryption is weak or poorly implemented.

🔑 **Hashcat / John the Ripper** – Used to crack weak authentication keys.

📺 **Side-Channel Attacks** – Monitors power consumption or timing patterns to infer cryptographic keys.

🔍 **Known-Plaintext Attacks** – Used when part of the encrypted message is known, making it easier to derive the key.

🚀 **Example**: A group of researchers once brute-forced an old GPS satellite's encryption algorithm in under 24 hours, proving that certain military satellites were still using outdated security measures.

3. Exploiting Reverse-Engineered Satellite Protocols

Once an attacker understands a satellite protocol, the next step is exploitation. Here's what they can do:

A. Intercept & Modify Communications

If a satellite's data isn't properly encrypted, attackers can:

🔍 Eavesdrop on sensitive transmissions (e.g., weather data, military operations).
🎭 Inject false data into satellite feeds (e.g., spoof GPS signals).
📍 Replay past transmissions to trick ground stations into accepting fake telemetry.

🚀 **Example**: In 2020, security researchers demonstrated that certain weather satellites were broadcasting unencrypted imagery, meaning anyone with an SDR could intercept and modify satellite weather data.

B. Hijack Command and Control Signals

By mimicking valid protocol commands, hackers could:

☐ Alter a satellite's orbit or payload settings.
☐ Disrupt satellite operations by sending conflicting commands.
☐ Trigger self-destruct or fail-safe mechanisms (not all satellites have them, but some do).

🚀 **Example**: The 1999 UK "SkyNet" Satellite Incident was suspected to be a protocol hijacking attack, where unknown hackers sent rogue commands that disabled military satellite communications.

C. Inject Malicious Firmware or Software

Once inside a system, attackers could modify the satellite's firmware to:

☐☐ Install persistent backdoors for future access.
🏯 Reroute data transmissions to unauthorized receivers.
☐ Prevent ground stations from regaining control of the satellite.

🚀 **Example**: A group of ethical hackers once proved that certain commercial satellites were vulnerable to firmware injection attacks, allowing attackers to completely take over the satellite.

4. Defending Against Protocol-Based Attacks

So how do we stop hackers from pulling off these attacks? Here are some best practices:

✅ **Encrypt All Satellite Communications** – Ensure data and command channels use strong encryption.
✅ **Implement Authentication for Commands** – Require cryptographic signatures for all satellite control instructions.
✅ **Use Intrusion Detection Systems (IDS)** – Monitor for unusual transmission patterns.
✅ **Regularly Audit Firmware & Protocol Implementations** – Check for vulnerabilities before deployment.
✅ **Limit Access to Satellite Transmissions** – Use frequency hopping or spread spectrum techniques to make eavesdropping harder.

Final Thoughts: Hacking Satellites is Hard… But Not Impossible 🚀

Reverse engineering proprietary satellite protocols isn't easy, but with the right tools and knowledge, it's definitely possible. And as we've seen, many satellite networks still rely on outdated security measures—making them prime targets for cyberattacks.

If aerospace companies want to keep their satellites safe, they need to take security seriously—because if a group of hackers in their basement can decode your satellite's protocol, imagine what a well-funded nation-state attacker could do. ☐

8.4 Injecting Backdoors and Modifying Satellite Operations

Hacking Satellites: Because Regular Wi-Fi Networks Were Too Easy

There's something uniquely terrifying—and thrilling—about the idea of injecting a backdoor into a satellite. Forget hacking your neighbor's Wi-Fi or messing with IoT light bulbs—this is next-level cyber mischief. With a well-placed backdoor, an attacker could:

🚀 Take control of satellite communications
📡 Modify or redirect data transmissions
☐ Lock out legitimate operators (because why share?)
🔥 Trigger a deorbit sequence (okay, let's not get too wild here...)

Unlike traditional network hacking, where you exploit a vulnerable web server or phish some poor IT guy, hacking satellites requires deep knowledge of space systems, RF communications, and firmware security. But once you're in? You own that flying chunk of metal. Let's talk about how attackers do it—and how to stop them.

1. What is a Backdoor in a Satellite?

A backdoor is any hidden or unauthorized access point that allows an attacker to bypass normal security controls. In satellites, these can be:

💡 **Firmware-Based Backdoors** – Malicious modifications in the satellite's software.
📡 **Communication Backdoors** – Hidden command interfaces that respond to special signals.
⚲ **Hardware Backdoors** – Pre-installed vulnerabilities in chips or circuits (sometimes placed there intentionally by manufacturers or nation-states).

Hackers (or rogue insiders) can install these before launch (during development) or after deployment (via over-the-air updates or hijacking ground control systems).

🚀 **Real-World Example**: In 1998, hackers allegedly took control of U.S.-German ROSAT X-ray satellite by gaining access to ground control and pointing its solar panels directly at the Sun, effectively frying its batteries and rendering it useless. A backdoor in the system could have prevented engineers from regaining control.

2. How Backdoors Get Planted in Satellite Systems

Hackers love finding and inserting backdoors into satellite systems, and they have multiple ways of doing it:

A. Exploiting Vulnerabilities in Ground Control Software

Ground stations send commands to satellites, and if those systems are vulnerable, an attacker can hijack them.

☐ **Attack Method:**

Exploit weak authentication in ground control software.

Use stolen credentials or phishing attacks against satellite operators.

Inject malicious software updates to gain persistent access.

🔥 **Example**: In 2007 and 2008, attackers hijacked Landsat-7 and Terra AM-1 satellites for several minutes by compromising ground station systems. No damage was reported, but it was a wake-up call.

B. Firmware Tampering & Malicious Updates

Satellites receive firmware updates to fix bugs and add features. But if these updates aren't secure, an attacker can inject a backdoor directly into the satellite's operating system.

☐ **Attack Method:**

Capture a legitimate firmware update, modify it, and resend it.

Exploit weaknesses in update authentication.

Install malicious code that allows remote access or logs keystrokes.

🔥 **Example**: In 2022, security researchers demonstrated how some commercial satellites lacked proper firmware signing, meaning anyone who intercepted an update could modify and re-upload it.

C. Exploiting Poorly Secured Communication Channels

Many satellites still use outdated encryption—or no encryption at all—to communicate. If an attacker intercepts a transmission, they can:

🗡 Replay old commands (making the satellite think it received a legitimate signal).
🔍 Inject rogue instructions to modify operations.
☐ Jam or disrupt legitimate communications, preventing recovery.

🔥 **Example**: In 2014, researchers discovered that certain DVB-S broadcast satellites were transmitting unencrypted control commands, making them vulnerable to spoofing.

3. Modifying Satellite Operations: What Can an Attacker Do?

Once a hacker has backdoor access to a satellite, they can pull off some seriously dangerous tricks.

A. Manipulating Data Transmission

Attackers can alter satellite data before it reaches Earth:

📷 Modify surveillance images (blur out military assets or insert fake objects).
📊 Change weather data (useful for manipulating forecasts or disaster response).
🗡 Reroute transmissions (send critical data to an unauthorized receiver).

🔥 **Example**: In 2018, security experts warned that hacked weather satellites could be used to manipulate financial markets by faking storm data.

B. Orbit & Attitude Manipulation

If an attacker gains control over a satellite's thrusters and positioning systems, they could:

🚀 Alter its orbit (moving it into a useless trajectory).
☐ Disrupt other satellites (bumping into neighbors—yes, this has happened).
🔥 Deorbit it entirely (forcing it to re-enter Earth's atmosphere and burn up).

🔥 **Example**: In 2019, a European Space Agency (ESA) satellite had to perform an emergency maneuver to avoid collision with a rogue SpaceX Starlink satellite that wasn't responding to commands—some speculated a cyberattack could have been involved.

C. Locking Out Legitimate Operators

If a hacker fully takes over a satellite, they can:

🔒 Change authentication keys, preventing ground control from regaining access.
☐ Disable safety mechanisms, making recovery impossible.
🔦 Demand ransom in exchange for returning control.

🔥 **Example**: In 1999, hackers allegedly took control of a British military satellite and demanded a ransom of nearly $1 million. The UK government denied it happened, but similar ransom-based attacks have been documented.

4. Defending Against Satellite Backdoor Attacks

If satellites are so vulnerable, how do we protect them? Here's what space agencies and cybersecurity experts recommend:

✅ **Implement Strong Firmware Signing & Authentication** – Ensure that only verified updates can be installed.
✅ **Encrypt All Communications** – Use end-to-end encryption to prevent command spoofing.
✅ **Harden Ground Station Security** – Patch vulnerabilities, use multi-factor authentication, and conduct regular security audits.
✅ **Implement AI-Based Anomaly Detection** – Use machine learning to detect unauthorized command patterns.
✅ **Limit Remote Access Capabilities** – Minimize unnecessary over-the-air control functions to reduce attack surfaces.

Final Thoughts: Satellites Are Cool... Until Hackers Take Over

Let's be honest—hacking satellites isn't just a cybersecurity issue. It's a national security issue. A well-placed backdoor in a critical satellite system could be used for espionage, sabotage, or even acts of war.

Space agencies and commercial satellite operators need to take security seriously, because as we've seen, attackers are already exploring these vulnerabilities. The difference between a secure satellite and a hacked one might just be a poorly configured access control list or an unpatched firmware exploit.

So, next time you look up at the night sky and see a satellite passing by, just remember—somewhere out there, someone might be trying to hack it. 🚀😺

8.5 Best Practices for Secure Satellite Firmware Development

Satellites Need Security Too—Because Space Hackers Are a Thing Now

Look, I get it—when people think of cybersecurity, they picture hoodie-clad hackers hunched over keyboards, cracking into Wi-Fi networks and stealing passwords. But what if I told you there are hackers trying to break into satellites? Yep, that shiny metal object orbiting Earth, beaming down GPS signals and internet connectivity, is just another target in the vast landscape of cyber threats.

And the best part? Some satellites still run decades-old firmware with little to no security updates. It's like trying to secure your modern banking app with a Windows 95 firewall—not a great idea. So, if we want to stop bad actors from brute-forcing, hijacking, or injecting backdoors into space systems, we need to start at the source: firmware security.

So buckle up, because today, we're talking about how to develop rock-solid, hacker-resistant firmware for satellites! 🚀💻

1. Why Satellite Firmware Security Matters

Satellite firmware is essentially the brain of a spacecraft. It controls:

Communications (uplink, downlink, and data transmission).

Attitude control (keeping the satellite properly aligned in space).

Payload operations (weather monitoring, GPS, internet services, etc.).

Security mechanisms (or, in some cases, the lack of them ☐).

Now, imagine what happens if a hacker compromises that firmware. They could:

☐ Lock out legitimate operators (yes, ransomware for satellites is a thing).
🗡 Intercept or alter communications (great for espionage).

🚀 Take control of thrusters (hello, accidental space collisions).

🔥 Shut down mission-critical functions (a nightmare for any space agency).

In short, weak firmware security = easy access for cybercriminals. And trust me, nobody wants to wake up one day and realize their expensive satellite is now the property of some rogue hacker group.

2. Best Practices for Secure Satellite Firmware Development

To keep satellites safe from cyber threats, developers need to follow some golden rules when designing firmware. Let's break them down:

A. Secure Boot and Code Signing

🚀 **Rule #1: If it's not signed, it's not getting in.**

One of the biggest mistakes developers make? Allowing unsigned firmware updates. That's like leaving your front door unlocked in a neighborhood full of burglars. Secure boot ensures that only authenticated firmware can run on the satellite.

✅ **Best Practices:**

✓ Enable cryptographic signing for all firmware updates (RSA, ECC, etc.).

✓ Use secure boot to verify the integrity of firmware before execution.

✓ Require multi-step verification for all firmware updates.

🔥 **Real-World Fail**: In 2019, researchers found that some commercial satellites didn't verify firmware updates, meaning anyone who intercepted an update could modify it and install malware. Not great.

B. Implement Strong Encryption for Data Storage and Transmission

🚀 **Rule #2: If it's readable, it's hackable.**

Some satellites still transmit unencrypted commands and telemetry data (I wish I were joking). That means anyone with a decent Software-Defined Radio (SDR) setup can intercept and manipulate these signals. Encrypt everything—always.

✅ Best Practices:

✔ Use AES-256 encryption for data at rest and in transit.

✔ Encrypt firmware updates to prevent tampering.

✔ Use authenticated key exchange protocols to prevent spoofing.

🔥 **Real-World Fail**: In 2014, security experts discovered that several satellite communication networks were transmitting sensitive data in plaintext, making them vulnerable to MITM attacks.

C. Reduce Attack Surface with Minimalist Code

🚀 **Rule #3: Less code = fewer bugs = fewer exploits.**

Every additional function, library, or module in firmware is a potential vulnerability. If your satellite doesn't need a certain feature, don't include it.

✅ Best Practices:

✔ Follow a minimalist approach—no unnecessary code.

✔ Remove default admin accounts or hardcoded credentials (seriously).

✔ Limit unnecessary debugging interfaces that could be exploited.

🔥 **Real-World Fail**: A 2018 satellite hack simulation showed that an unused diagnostic port on a ground station could be exploited to upload malicious firmware.

D. Regular Security Audits & Penetration Testing

🚀 **Rule #4: If you don't test it, hackers will.**

Many satellite operators never perform security audits or penetration tests on their firmware. That's like building a bank vault and never checking if the locks work. Test early, test often.

✅ Best Practices:

✓ Conduct firmware security audits before deployment.

✓ Simulate real-world cyberattacks to identify vulnerabilities.

✓ Implement a bug bounty program for white-hat hackers to find issues.

🔥 **Real-World Fail**: In 2020, hackers demonstrated how outdated firmware vulnerabilities in maritime satellite systems could be used to gain full control over communications.

E. Implement Firmware Rollback Protection

🚀 **Rule #5: No take-backs for attackers.**

If an attacker installs malicious firmware, they'll often rollback to an older, insecure version to maintain access. Prevent that.

✅ **Best Practices:**

✓ Use rollback prevention mechanisms to block older firmware.

✓ Log all firmware update attempts for forensic analysis.

✓ Require multi-factor authentication for firmware changes.

🔥 **Real-World Fail**: In 2017, attackers exploited a rollback vulnerability in industrial IoT systems, allowing them to install outdated firmware with known security flaws.

3. The Future of Satellite Firmware Security

As more companies and governments launch satellites into space, cybersecurity needs to be a top priority. Emerging technologies like AI-based anomaly detection, blockchain for secure firmware updates, and quantum encryption will play a key role in future defenses.

But no matter how advanced technology gets, the fundamental principles remain the same:

🚀 Secure boot.
🚀 Strong encryption.

🚀 Minimalist code.
🚀 Regular security testing.
🚀 Rollback protection.

The reality is satellite hacking is no longer science fiction—it's a real and growing threat. And if we don't start treating firmware security like the mission-critical issue it is, we'll be seeing a lot more "unintended" space accidents.

Final Thoughts: Do You Want Hackers Controlling Satellites? No? Secure Your Firmware.

The bottom line? Satellites are awesome, but they're also juicy cyber targets. Whether it's for espionage, financial gain, or just plain mischief, attackers love weakly secured firmware—so don't give them an easy win.

If you're developing satellite firmware, do it right. And if you're just here to learn how hackers break into satellites—well, at least now you know what to look for. 🚀😼

Chapter 9: Offensive Use of Satellites and Military Cyberwarfare

Picture this: a nation-state hacker, sitting in a dark room, launching a cyberattack from orbit while sipping on an overpriced latte. Sounds like something out of a spy thriller, right? Well, space-based cyberwarfare is very real, and governments around the world are already leveraging satellites for espionage, disruption, and even potential attacks.

This chapter delves into the offensive use of satellite technology in cyberwarfare, covering tactics like satellite-based intelligence gathering, jamming enemy communications, and launching cyberattacks from space assets. We'll examine case studies of alleged satellite hacking incidents and discuss strategies for defending against nation-state cyber threats in the space domain.

9.1 Weaponizing Satellites for Cyber and Physical Attacks

Satellites: From Science Fiction to Real-World Cyber Weapons

Once upon a time, satellites were just peaceful, floating hunks of metal that did things like transmit TV signals, provide GPS, and help predict the weather. But now? They're prime cyber warfare assets, capable of spying, hacking, jamming, and even attacking physical infrastructure.

That's right—real-life "killer satellites" exist, and they're not just in Hollywood movies. Governments, militaries, and even rogue hackers are exploring ways to weaponize satellites, turning them into tools for cyber warfare, electronic attacks, and even kinetic destruction (yes, space lasers are a thing now).

So, let's dive into how satellites can be used as offensive cyber and physical weapons, why this is a growing threat, and what can be done to stop it. 🚀💀

1. How Satellites Can Be Weaponized

Weaponizing satellites doesn't mean strapping missiles to them (though some nations might be working on that). Instead, they can be used for:

A. Cyber Warfare and Espionage

🔍 **Spying and Intelligence Gathering** – Satellites already play a key role in surveillance, but compromised satellites can be used for covert data collection on a much larger scale. A hacked communications satellite could be used to eavesdrop on government or corporate data traffic.

💻 **Hacking and Network Disruption** – A compromised satellite could be used as a relay point for cybercriminals to launch attacks without leaving an obvious digital footprint. A nation-state actor could hijack a satellite to reroute or block internet traffic in targeted regions.

🔥 **Real-World Example**: In 2022, a cyberattack on Viasat disrupted satellite internet in Ukraine, allegedly as part of Russian military operations.

B. Electronic Warfare: Jamming and Spoofing

📡 **Jamming Communications** – An adversary could use satellites to jam military or civilian communication systems, cutting off internet, GPS, or emergency response networks.

🎭 **GPS Spoofing** – By transmitting false signals, a malicious satellite can manipulate GPS navigation systems, leading to misdirected military operations or civilian transport chaos.

🔥 **Real-World Example**: Reports suggest that GPS jamming and spoofing have been used in conflict zones to mislead drones and military vehicles.

C. Kinetic and Physical Attacks

🛰️ **Anti-Satellite (ASAT) Attacks** – Some countries have developed ASAT weapons capable of physically destroying satellites. This creates dangerous space debris that can damage other satellites and threaten space operations.

🚀 **Direct Energy and High-Powered Microwave (HPM) Attacks** – Satellites equipped with high-powered microwaves could potentially disable enemy electronics without needing a physical strike.

🔥 **Real-World Example**: The U.S., China, Russia, and India have all tested ASAT weapons, demonstrating their ability to destroy satellites with missiles.

2. Real-World Threats: Who's Doing What?

A. Nation-State Cyber Warfare

Countries like the U.S., China, Russia, and Iran have invested heavily in offensive satellite capabilities. Their strategies include:

Hacking enemy satellites to disrupt operations.

Using satellites as cyber weapons to launch digital attacks.

Deploying space-based jamming and spoofing technology.

🔥 **Example**: The U.S. Space Force was created partly to address the increasing weaponization of satellites and protect American space assets.

B. Private Sector and Rogue Actors

While nation-states dominate satellite warfare, private companies and even hackers are getting in on the action.

Corporate Espionage: Some corporations may try to hack competitor satellites to gain economic or strategic advantages.

Hacktivists: Groups like Anonymous have previously targeted satellite networks in protest of global policies.

Cybercriminals: Satellite hacking could be sold as a service on the dark web, similar to ransomware operations.

🔥 **Example**: In 2022, cybersecurity experts warned that ransomware gangs might start targeting satellites for ransom or sabotage.

3. Defending Against Weaponized Satellites

So, how do we protect space assets from cyber and physical threats?

A. Strengthening Satellite Cybersecurity

⬜⬜ **Encrypted Communications** – All satellite data links should be end-to-end encrypted to prevent interception.
⬜ **Regular Firmware Updates** – Just like any other IoT device, satellites need frequent security patches.
🔍 **Anomaly Detection AI** – AI-powered monitoring systems can detect suspicious activity or unauthorized access.

🔥 **Example**: The U.S. military has started using AI-powered cybersecurity for space assets to detect potential attacks before they happen.

B. Space-Based Threat Intelligence and Tracking

⬜⬜ **Space Surveillance Systems** – Governments and companies are investing in real-time satellite tracking to detect possible threats.
● **Early Warning Systems** – If an attack is detected, defensive measures like orbital maneuvers or countermeasures can be deployed.

🔥 **Example**: The U.S. Space Surveillance Network (SSN) tracks over 27,000 objects in orbit, including potential threats from hostile satellites.

C. International Space Cybersecurity Agreements

⬜ **Global Cooperation** – Nations must agree on cybersecurity policies for satellites, just like they do for nuclear weapons or chemical warfare.
🏛 **Space Treaties** – Updating treaties like the Outer Space Treaty to include cybersecurity guidelines.

🔥 **Example**: The United Nations has proposed new cybersecurity frameworks for satellites, but adoption has been slow.

Final Thoughts: The Future of Satellite Warfare

Weaponizing satellites is no longer a concept for sci-fi movies—it's happening right now. Whether it's cyber espionage, jamming attacks, or full-scale space warfare, the risks are real, and governments, corporations, and cybersecurity experts need to prepare.

The good news? Defensive strategies are evolving just as fast as offensive ones. With AI-powered threat detection, better encryption, and international cooperation, we can still keep space a secure (and hopefully, peaceful) domain.

But let's be real—if history has taught us anything, it's that every technological advancement eventually gets weaponized. The question isn't if satellites will be used in cyber warfare… it's how bad it will get before we take security seriously.

So, the next time you check Google Maps for directions or binge-watch Netflix via satellite internet, just remember—there's an entire war being fought in space, one cyberattack at a time. 🚀💀

9.2 Satellite-Based Espionage and Intelligence Gathering

Spying from Space: The Ultimate "I See You" Moment

Ever get the feeling that someone's watching you? Well, if you're outside, congratulations—you might actually be right! Satellites have been quietly keeping an eye on everything from military bases to fast food drive-thrus (okay, maybe not that last one… or maybe 👀).

But let's get serious—satellite-based espionage is one of the most powerful tools in modern intelligence. Governments, corporations, and even rogue actors leverage satellites to monitor global activities, track movements, intercept communications, and even predict geopolitical events before they happen. If you thought the NSA had good listening skills, wait until you learn about spy satellites.

So, how exactly do satellites become the ultimate surveillance tool? Let's break it down.

1. The Many Ways Satellites Spy on Us

Satellite espionage isn't just about zooming in on top-secret bases like in the movies (although, yeah, that's definitely a thing). It involves multiple intelligence-gathering techniques, including:

A. Optical and Infrared Surveillance

🛰️ **High-Resolution Imaging** – Modern satellites can capture images so detailed they can identify a car's license plate from orbit. Some even see through camouflage and cloud cover.

🔥 **Example**: The U.S. KH-11 reconnaissance satellites, nicknamed "Keyhole," can reportedly capture images with resolutions down to 10 cm per pixel. That means they can read your newspaper if you're holding it outside.

◻◻ **Infrared Sensors** – These allow satellites to detect heat signatures, making it easy to track missile launches, hidden military bases, and even underground bunkers.

🔥 **Example**: The U.S. Space-Based Infrared System (SBIRS) constantly monitors for heat plumes from ballistic missile launches.

B. Electronic Signal Interception (SIGINT & COMINT)

📡 **Listening to Enemy Communications** – Spy satellites can eavesdrop on radio, cellular, and military transmissions, intercepting everything from diplomatic calls to encrypted military signals.

📶 **Tracking Radar and Missile Systems** – Satellites can map enemy radar installations, allowing militaries to identify weaknesses and blind spots in air defense systems.

🔥 **Example**: The USA-278 Orion satellite, operated by the NSA, is rumored to capture enemy military communications across vast regions.

C. GPS Tracking and Monitoring Movement

◻◻ Watching Military Convoys and Naval Fleets – Governments use satellites to track troop movements, identify fleet locations, and predict enemy strategies.

🚗 **Civilian Tracking**? Maybe. Some experts believe intelligence agencies could leverage satellites to track individuals, especially those using GPS-enabled devices.

🔥 **Example**: The National Reconnaissance Office (NRO), which operates most U.S. spy satellites, plays a major role in tracking global military and terrorist movements.

D. Cyber Espionage via Satellites

🖥 **Intercepting Data Traffic** – Some satellites are capable of tapping into internet traffic relayed through space, giving attackers access to emails, messages, and sensitive data.

🚀 **Spoofing Satellite Signals** – Intelligence agencies have experimented with manipulating satellite signals to mislead enemy forces or track cybercriminal activities.

🔥 **Example**: China and Russia have been accused of developing satellite-based cyber warfare tactics, including the ability to intercept or jam foreign military communications.

2. The Players: Who's Spying on Whom?

A. The Usual Suspects (U.S., China, Russia, EU)

Major global powers all have classified reconnaissance satellite programs, used for both defense and espionage.

US **The U.S.** – Operates some of the most advanced spy satellites, including KH-11, Orion, and SBIRS, used for global surveillance and military intelligence.

CN **China** – Runs the Yaogan satellite network, capable of high-resolution imaging, electronic surveillance, and tracking U.S. naval fleets in the Pacific.

RU **Russia** – Uses Kosmos reconnaissance satellites for spying on NATO military operations.

EU **European Union** – The Copernicus and Helios programs provide satellite intelligence for European military operations.

🔥 **Example**: Leaked documents from Edward Snowden revealed that the U.S. used satellites to intercept millions of phone calls worldwide under the PRISM and ECHELON programs.

B. Private Companies in the Espionage Game

Governments aren't the only ones with powerful satellites—private companies are joining the game.

Maxar Technologies – Provides high-resolution imagery for military and commercial intelligence.

Planet Labs – Operates over 200 mini-satellites, offering near real-time Earth observation.

SpaceX's Starlink? – Some speculate that Starlink's vast network could be leveraged for intelligence gathering.

🔥 **Example**: In 2022, commercial satellites from Maxar and Planet Labs were used to track Russian troop movements before the invasion of Ukraine.

3. Countermeasures: Can You Hide from Satellites?

If you're an average person, you're probably not important enough to be spied on from space. But for governments and organizations? Avoiding satellite surveillance is a serious challenge.

A. Camouflage and Deception

Heat Decoys – Some military bases use fake heat signatures to mislead infrared satellites.

Electronic Warfare – Militaries deploy jamming devices to block signal interception.

Moving Equipment at Night – Troops and vehicles sometimes move under cloud cover to avoid optical satellites.

🔥 **Example**: The U.S. uses fake aircraft carriers in satellite images to deceive enemy intelligence agencies.

B. Anti-Satellite (ASAT) Weapons

Some nations have developed ASAT missiles to shoot down spy satellites if necessary.

🔥 **Example**: In 2007, China destroyed one of its own satellites in an ASAT test, creating a dangerous cloud of space debris.

C. Cybersecurity for Satellite Communications

Encrypted Satellite Data – Prevents interception of military and corporate satellite transmissions.

Quantum Cryptography – Some nations are testing unhackable quantum communication via satellites.

🔥 **Example**: In 2017, China launched the Micius quantum satellite, capable of sending encrypted messages that can't be intercepted.

Final Thoughts: The Future of Satellite Espionage

As satellites get more advanced, cheaper, and more accessible, satellite espionage is no longer limited to governments. From military spying to corporate surveillance, space-based intelligence is only growing.

So, next time you're outside waving at the sky, just remember—someone might actually be watching. 👀 🛰️

9.3 Space-Based Cyberwarfare Tactics and Nation-State Threats

War in Space: Because Hacking the Planet Wasn't Enough

Remember when space was all about moon landings, cool rovers, and dreaming about intergalactic travel? Yeah, those were the good old days. Now, space is another battlefield, and satellites are the high-value targets of modern cyberwarfare. Nation-states aren't just launching satellites for scientific discovery anymore—they're hacking, jamming, and even considering outright destruction of their rivals' space assets.

Welcome to the wild, wild west of space cybersecurity, where nations are using code instead of bullets and satellites instead of tanks. If you've ever thought, "What's the worst that could happen if someone hacked a satellite?", well... let's just say it starts with espionage and ends with potential global chaos.

So, how are nation-states using space-based cyberwarfare tactics, and what does this mean for the future of satellite security? Let's take a deep dive into the real Star Wars—no lightsabers, just firewalls (hopefully).

1. How Satellites Become Cyberwarfare Targets

Satellites are prime real estate in cyberwarfare for one simple reason: they are high-value assets that control everything from military operations to internet access. Disrupting or hijacking them gives a nation-state a strategic advantage without ever firing a missile. Here's how:

A. Command & Control Takeovers

Some satellites still run on outdated and poorly secured protocols, making them vulnerable to full-blown hijacking. If a hacker (or a hostile government) gains access to the command system, they can:

Shut down or disable the satellite

Redirect it to a different mission (like pointing a surveillance satellite away from key areas)

Use it for espionage or misinformation campaigns

🔥 **Example**: In 1998, hackers took control of ROSAT, a German X-ray satellite, and permanently disabled its solar panels, ultimately destroying the satellite.

B. Signal Jamming & Spoofing

Satellites depend on clean communication signals to function properly. Cyberwarfare tactics like jamming and spoofing can render them useless or even trick them into sending false data.

Jamming – Flooding the satellite's signal with noise, effectively blocking communication between the satellite and ground stations.

Spoofing – Sending fake signals to make the satellite believe incorrect data is real, leading to disastrous consequences.

🔥 **Example**: In 2011, Iran claimed to have hijacked a U.S. RQ-170 drone by using GPS spoofing—a tactic that could be used against satellites as well.

C. Malware in Space Systems

Yes, even satellites can get infected with malware. If a satellite's ground station or software update process is compromised, an attacker can deploy malicious code to:

Intercept and steal data

Corrupt mission-critical functions

Launch coordinated cyberattacks on Earth-based infrastructure

🔥 **Example**: In 2022, just hours before Russia's invasion of Ukraine, a massive cyberattack disabled Viasat satellite modems, disrupting communications across Europe.

D. Physical Attacks on Satellites

When cyberwarfare isn't enough, some nations resort to physical destruction of enemy satellites using:

Anti-satellite (ASAT) missiles – Literal satellite assassinations.

Directed energy weapons – Yes, laser attacks on satellites are a real thing.

Kinetic Kill Vehicles (KKVs) – Basically, crashing a satellite into another at high speed.

🔥 **Example**: In 2007, China destroyed one of its own satellites with an ASAT missile, sending a message to the world that space warfare is no longer theoretical.

2. The Nation-State Players in Space Cyberwarfare

A. United States US

The U.S. leads in satellite cybersecurity and space dominance, but it also has the most satellites to defend.

Space Force (yes, it's real) – A military branch dedicated to defending U.S. space assets.

X-37B Spaceplane – A secretive orbital vehicle that many believe is involved in cyberwarfare research.

Offensive Cyber Capabilities – The U.S. has openly admitted that it has satellite hacking and counter-hacking programs.

🔥 **Example**: The U.S. Cyber Command (USCYBERCOM) runs cyber operations that include defending against space-based threats.

B. China CN

China has rapidly developed both offensive and defensive space cyberwarfare capabilities.

Yaogan Satellites – Used for reconnaissance, but potentially cyber-attack capable.

Quantum Satellite Communications – Developing hacker-proof encryption for military communications.

GPS Spoofing and Jamming Research – Allegedly used in naval exercises to mislead foreign forces.

🔥 **Example**: The Tiangong Space Station is rumored to have advanced cyber capabilities for space-based defense and offense.

C. Russia RU

Russia has some of the most aggressive cyberwarfare capabilities, including satellite-based operations.

Electronic Warfare Units – Capable of disrupting satellite signals over Europe.

Hacking into Space Agencies – Linked to cyberattacks on NASA, ESA, and other agencies.

ASAT Missile Tests – Conducted in 2021, causing major international backlash.

🔥 **Example**: The NotPetya malware attack in 2017 was allegedly tied to Russian cyberwarfare tactics, showing their ability to take down global infrastructure.

D. Other Emerging Threats ☐

North Korea – Developing missile and cyber capabilities that could threaten satellites.

Iran – Experimenting with satellite jamming and GPS manipulation.

Private Corporations – Companies like SpaceX and Amazon's Project Kuiper could become targets or players in space cyberwarfare.

3. Defending Against Space Cyberwarfare

So, how do we stop nation-states from turning space into a full-blown battlefield? The defense strategies include:

A. Hardening Satellite Security

Better Encryption – Upgrading to quantum-resistant cryptography to prevent data theft.

Redundant Control Systems – Backup communication pathways in case of an attack.

Real-Time Threat Detection – AI-powered monitoring to identify cyber intrusions.

🔥 **Example**: The U.S. is investing in SpaceX's Starshield program, which could provide hardened military satellite communications.

B. International Space Cybersecurity Treaties

Right now, space laws are way behind space technology. Nations need to work together to:

Ban cyberattacks on civilian satellites

Develop international response protocols for space-based cyber incidents

Limit the weaponization of space cybersecurity technologies

🔥 **Example**: The Outer Space Treaty (1967) prevents nuclear weapons in space but says nothing about cyberwarfare.

Final Thoughts: The Future of Cyberwar in Space

Cyberwarfare is no longer limited to Earth-based networks—it has officially moved to space. Nation-states know the strategic value of satellites, and as hacking tools become more advanced, attacks on space infrastructure will only increase.

The future of satellite cybersecurity depends on defensive innovation, international cooperation, and maybe—just maybe—convincing world leaders that hacking satellites isn't the best way to resolve their disagreements.

But let's be real… when has that ever worked? 🚀😊

9.4 Case Studies: Alleged Satellite Hacking Incidents (China, Russia, US)

Hacking Satellites: Because Cybercriminals Wanted to Go Intergalactic

You'd think hacking satellites would be something straight out of a Hollywood sci-fi movie, right? Some rogue genius in a dark basement, wearing a hoodie, typing furiously as the screen flashes "ACCESS GRANTED", and suddenly—boom!—the ISS is playing Rick Astley's Never Gonna Give You Up on loop.

Well, reality is even crazier. Satellite hacking isn't just a fantasy; it has allegedly happened multiple times, involving some of the most powerful nations in the world. We're talking about real incidents where satellites were jammed, hijacked, or outright disabled—sometimes for espionage, sometimes for political leverage, and sometimes just because they could.

Let's look at three of the most notorious alleged satellite hacking incidents, where China, Russia, and the U.S. were all accused of not-so-friendly cyber activities in space.

1. China: The Alleged Hack of U.S. Weather Satellites (2007-2008)

The Accusation:

Between 2007 and 2008, two U.S. government satellites—Terra EOS and Landsat-7—were allegedly hacked through a compromised ground station in Norway. Reports suggest that hackers linked to China gained control over satellite functions for minutes at a time.

How It Happened:

The attack was traced back to a ground station in Svalbard, Norway.

Hackers exploited vulnerabilities in networked systems controlling the satellites.

They allegedly gained enough control to issue commands, though there's no public evidence they did anything destructive.

The Response:

The U.S. never officially confirmed that China was behind it, but intelligence reports pointed fingers at Chinese state-sponsored hackers.

This led to increased security in U.S. satellite systems and more scrutiny of China's cyberwarfare capabilities.

Why It Matters:

If true, this attack demonstrated that foreign actors could remotely hijack satellites.

It raised concerns that future cyberattacks could manipulate satellite data, disrupt military operations, or even cause collisions in orbit.

🔥 **Fun Fact**: China has since developed its own satellite network, possibly to avoid being on the receiving end of a similar attack.

2. Russia: The Viasat Cyberattack (2022)

The Accusation:

On February 24, 2022—just hours before Russia's invasion of Ukraine—a massive cyberattack targeted Viasat's KA-SAT network, which provides satellite internet services across Europe. The attack disrupted communications in Ukraine and affected users across several countries.

How It Happened:

Hackers exploited the satellite's ground-based infrastructure, not the satellite itself.

They deployed malware to wipe modems, rendering them useless.

The attack was so widespread that even remote wind farms in Germany lost connectivity.

The Response:

The U.S., EU, and UK blamed Russia, stating the attack was meant to cripple Ukrainian military communications.

Viasat and cybersecurity firms worked to restore service and distribute new modems.

The attack is now considered one of the first major satellite cyberwarfare operations.

Why It Matters:

This event proved that satellite networks are critical wartime targets.

It showed that disrupting internet infrastructure from space could become a common warfare tactic.

🔥 **Fun Fact**: The attack accidentally affected thousands of civilian users in Europe, proving that cyberwarfare doesn't always go as planned.

3. U.S.: Alleged Hacking of Russian Satellites (2015-Present)

The Accusation:

Russia has accused the U.S. of attempting to infiltrate and disrupt its satellite communications on multiple occasions. While details are murky, Russian officials have suggested that:

The U.S. has conducted cyber espionage on Russian space assets.

Russian satellite signals have been interfered with or spoofed.

There were attempts to access Russian military satellite systems.

How It Happened (Allegedly):

The U.S. has some of the most advanced cyberwarfare capabilities, meaning an attack on Russian satellites would likely involve:

Signal interception for intelligence gathering.

Software-based intrusions into satellite control systems.

GPS spoofing to mislead navigation satellites.

The Response:

Russia has ramped up efforts to protect its space assets through encryption and better cybersecurity.

The country has also developed counter-space capabilities, including anti-satellite (ASAT) weapons.

Why It Matters:

Russia's allegations suggest that cyberwarfare in space is not just theoretical—it's an active battlefield.

The growing tension between nations raises concerns about potential escalation into full-scale space conflicts.

🔥 **Fun Fact**: Russia has publicly demonstrated GPS spoofing capabilities in places like Moscow and the Black Sea, leading some to speculate they might have tested the same methods on satellites.

What These Cases Mean for the Future of Satellite Security

1. Cyberattacks on Satellites Are Becoming More Common

These cases prove that hacking satellites isn't science fiction anymore—it's happening right now.

With more nations and private companies launching satellites, cyber threats will continue to evolve.

2. Ground Stations Are the Weakest Link

In all three cases, the attacks targeted ground-based systems, not the satellites themselves.

This highlights the need for better security on Earth to protect assets in space.

3. Nation-States Are Investing Heavily in Space Cyberwarfare

The U.S., China, and Russia are all developing space-focused cybersecurity divisions.

Expect to see new treaties, regulations, and countermeasures in the coming years.

4. Satellites Need Stronger Encryption and Security Controls

Implementing quantum-resistant encryption and AI-driven threat detection could help prevent future attacks.

Multi-layered security, including redundant communication links, is becoming essential.

Final Thoughts: Welcome to the Space Cyberwar Era

So, what did we learn today?

Yes, satellites can be hacked.

Yes, some of the world's biggest powers are already doing it.

Yes, space cyberwarfare is just getting started.

With more companies like SpaceX, Amazon, and China's CASC launching their own mega-constellations, the attack surface is only getting bigger and juicier for cybercriminals and nation-state hackers.

Space isn't just about exploration anymore—it's about domination, security, and the never-ending chess game of cyberwarfare. Buckle up, folks. The final frontier just became the next battlefield. 🚀😊

9.5 Defending Against Offensive Cyber Operations in Space

Cyberwar in Space? I Didn't Sign Up for This!

Look, I love space as much as the next person. I grew up watching Star Wars and dreaming about flying an X-Wing. But let's be real—space has officially become the next cyber battlefield, and instead of laser battles, we've got satellites getting hacked, communications getting jammed, and nations flexing their cyber muscles.

If you think this is all sci-fi paranoia, think again. We've already seen real-world satellite cyberattacks, from the alleged Chinese breach of U.S. weather satellites to Russia's Viasat cyberattack in Ukraine. The reality? Satellites are highly vulnerable, and hackers—from criminal groups to nation-state actors—are actively trying to exploit them.

So, how do we fight back? How do we secure space assets against offensive cyber operations? That's exactly what we're diving into. Strap in—it's time to talk defense!

1. Understanding the Threat Landscape

Before we start securing satellites, we need to understand the types of attacks we're dealing with. Offensive cyber operations in space generally fall into a few categories:

Satellite Hijacking: Hackers take control of a satellite, potentially altering its orbit, disrupting its functions, or shutting it down completely.

Jamming and Spoofing: Attackers disrupt or manipulate satellite signals to cause communication failures or GPS misinformation.

Cyber Espionage: State-sponsored hackers intercept sensitive satellite data for intelligence-gathering.

Destructive Cyberattacks: Malicious actors use malware, DDoS attacks, or even physical destruction (like anti-satellite missiles) to disable space assets.

Each of these threats requires a different defense strategy, so let's break it down.

2. Hardening Satellite Security: Defense Strategies

A. Stronger Encryption for Satellite Communications

One of the easiest ways to protect satellite data is to ensure all transmissions are encrypted end-to-end. Yet, shockingly, many satellites still use outdated or weak encryption methods (some even lack encryption altogether—seriously?!).

Defense Measures:

✓ **Implement quantum-resistant encryption**: With quantum computing on the horizon, traditional encryption methods will eventually become obsolete. Space agencies need to future-proof their encryption now.

✅ **Use frequency hopping and spread spectrum techniques**: This makes it harder for attackers to intercept or jam signals.

✅ **Encrypt satellite control links**: Unauthorized access to satellite command systems can lead to catastrophic consequences. Lock it down!

B. Securing Ground Stations: The Weakest Link

Most cyberattacks on satellites don't target the satellites themselves—they hit ground stations. Why? Because ground stations are connected to the internet, making them vulnerable to hacking, malware, and insider threats.

Defense Measures:

✅ **Air-gap critical satellite control systems**: If hackers can't reach it via the internet, they can't hack it. Simple.

✅ **Use zero-trust architecture**: No one—not even internal employees—should have unrestricted access to satellite control systems.

✅ **Harden network security**: Deploy firewalls, intrusion detection systems, and strict access controls.

C. Detecting and Preventing Satellite Hijacking

A hijacked satellite is a national security nightmare. Imagine if an attacker takes over a military or navigation satellite—the consequences could be devastating.

Defense Measures:

✅ **Multi-factor authentication (MFA) for satellite commands**: No single user should have the ability to execute critical commands.

✅ **AI-powered anomaly detection**: Machine learning can identify unusual activity (e.g., unauthorized access attempts, sudden command changes) and flag them in real time.

✅ **Fail-safe command protocols**: Implement kill switches or recovery protocols that allow operators to regain control if a satellite is compromised.

D. Defending Against Jamming and Spoofing Attacks

Jamming and spoofing attacks can disrupt communications, interfere with GPS signals, and mislead navigation systems—a huge risk for military, aviation, and financial sectors.

Defense Measures:

✅ **Directional antennas and beamforming**: These help satellites focus signals in specific directions, making them harder to jam.

✅ **Anti-jamming technologies**: Techniques like adaptive filtering and frequency hopping can counter jamming attacks.

✅ **GNSS authentication**: Secure GPS signals with cryptographic authentication to prevent spoofing.

3. The Role of AI and Machine Learning in Space Cybersecurity

Artificial intelligence is becoming a game-changer for cybersecurity—and space is no exception. AI-driven security systems can:

Monitor satellite traffic in real-time to detect anomalies.

Predict potential threats based on past attack patterns.

Automate responses to cyber incidents, reducing human intervention time.

Space agencies and private companies like SpaceX, Amazon's Project Kuiper, and China's CASC are already exploring AI-based security solutions.

4. International Collaboration: A Space Cybersecurity Alliance?

Cybersecurity in space isn't just a tech issue—it's a political one. The lack of global regulations makes it easier for nation-state hackers to operate in the shadows.

Some potential solutions include:

☐ **International cybersecurity treaties for space assets** – Similar to arms control agreements, but for satellites.

☐ **Information-sharing between nations and private companies** – Transparency can help counteract threats more effectively.

⚖️☐ **Stronger legal consequences for satellite cyberattacks** – Holding cybercriminals accountable on an international level.

5. The Future of Space Cyber Defense

As satellites become more critical to global infrastructure, military operations, and everyday life, the importance of defending them against cyber threats will only grow. The future of space cybersecurity might include:

🚀 **Quantum communication satellites** – Secure messaging using quantum entanglement to make eavesdropping impossible.
🔲🔲 **Self-healing AI-driven satellites** – Satellites that can detect attacks and automatically restore themselves.
🔒 **Blockchain-based satellite security** – Distributed, tamper-proof security mechanisms for satellite control.

Final Thoughts: Space Ain't Just for Astronauts Anymore

When I got into cybersecurity, I never thought I'd be writing about hacking satellites. Yet, here we are—living in a world where cyberwarfare extends beyond Earth's atmosphere.

The bottom line? Space cybersecurity is no longer optional—it's a necessity. Whether you're a government agency, a private company, or an ethical hacker looking to make a difference, securing satellites should be a top priority.

So next time you look up at the night sky, just remember: those twinkling lights might be under attack right now.

Now, if you'll excuse me, I'm off to see if I can convince Elon Musk to encrypt Starlink better. 🚀😂

Chapter 10: Securing the Future of Space IoT and Satellite Systems

We've spent this whole book talking about how satellites can be hacked. Now let's talk about how to stop it—because, let's face it, a hacked satellite can cause way more damage than a hacked smart fridge (unless your fridge is launching nukes, in which case… we have bigger problems).

This chapter focuses on best practices for securing satellite systems, from implementing quantum encryption to leveraging AI-powered threat detection. We'll explore international collaboration efforts, emerging security frameworks, and future trends in satellite cybersecurity, ensuring that the next generation of space technology is built with security at its core.

10.1 Best Practices for Satellite Cybersecurity and Threat Mitigation

Securing Space: Because "Oops" Doesn't Work in Orbit

Look, I love a good cybersecurity challenge. Breaking into a network, testing defenses, and making things stronger—it's what gets me out of bed in the morning (well, that and coffee). But when it comes to satellites, the stakes are just a little bit higher. If your Wi-Fi gets hacked, it's annoying. If a satellite gets hacked, entire communication networks, military operations, and global navigation systems could go haywire.

And trust me, hackers are getting creative. We've seen satellite hijacking, GPS spoofing, data interception, and even cyberattacks that shut down entire fleets of space assets. So, what can we do? Simple—build stronger defenses and make life miserable for cybercriminals trying to poke holes in our space systems. In this chapter, we're diving into the best practices for securing satellites and keeping the bad guys out.

1. Secure Satellite Design: Start With Cybersecurity, Not as an Afterthought

One of the biggest mistakes companies make? Treating cybersecurity as an add-on instead of baking it into the design from the start. This is how we end up with satellites that:

Use weak encryption (or no encryption at all □).

Have hardcoded passwords that attackers can easily exploit.

Run outdated software with unpatched vulnerabilities.

To avoid these pitfalls, satellite manufacturers should:

✅ **Use secure-by-design principles** – Build cybersecurity into the hardware and software from day one.
✅ **Avoid hardcoded credentials** – If a password is baked into the firmware, hackers will find it.
✅ **Implement secure boot processes** – Only allow trusted software to run on satellite systems.
✅ **Use redundancy and fail-safe mechanisms** – If a satellite gets compromised, have a way to regain control or shut it down safely.

2. Encrypt Everything: Communications, Data, and Control Signals

Satellites send and receive massive amounts of sensitive data, from weather patterns to military intelligence. If this data isn't properly encrypted, attackers can intercept, manipulate, or disrupt it.

Best Practices for Encryption:

🔒 **End-to-end encryption** – Ensure data is encrypted from the moment it leaves a satellite until it reaches the ground station.
🔒 **Quantum-resistant cryptography** – With quantum computing on the horizon, traditional encryption will soon be vulnerable. Future-proof security now.
🔒 **Encrypt control signals** – If an attacker can send unauthorized commands, they could hijack a satellite. Secure it!

3. Secure Ground Stations: The Real Weak Link

Most cyberattacks on satellites don't start in space—they start on Earth. Ground stations, which control satellites and process their data, are often the most vulnerable part of the system. If a hacker compromises a ground station, they can:

Disrupt satellite communications.

Hijack control of the satellite.

Launch further attacks on global infrastructure.

How to Lock Down Ground Stations:

✓ **Isolate critical systems** – Keep mission-critical satellite controls on an air-gapped network (i.e., not connected to the internet).
✓ **Use multi-factor authentication (MFA)** – Even NASA got hacked due to weak authentication—don't make the same mistake.
✓ **Regularly patch and update software** – Unpatched vulnerabilities are an open door for hackers.

4. Prevent Jamming and Spoofing Attacks

Jamming and spoofing attacks are among the most common satellite threats. Jamming disrupts satellite signals, while spoofing tricks receivers into believing false information. The result? Navigation failures, communication blackouts, and even military disorientation.

How to Defend Against Jamming and Spoofing:

☐☐ **Use directional antennas** – Beamforming technology makes it harder for attackers to interfere with signals.
☐☐ **Deploy anti-jamming techniques** – Frequency hopping, spread spectrum communication, and adaptive filtering can help mitigate jamming.
☐☐ **Authenticate GPS signals** – Cryptographic authentication helps prevent GPS spoofing attacks.

5. AI-Powered Threat Detection: Your Space Security Sidekick

Hackers aren't working 9-to-5 jobs, so satellite security needs 24/7 monitoring. This is where artificial intelligence (AI) and machine learning (ML) come into play. AI-driven security systems can:

☐ Monitor satellite traffic in real-time and flag suspicious activity.
☐ Detect anomalies in command signals that might indicate a cyberattack.
☐ Automate threat response, reducing the need for human intervention.

The future of satellite cybersecurity is AI-driven, and companies like SpaceX, Lockheed Martin, and government agencies are already investing in AI-powered defenses.

6. Create an Incident Response Plan: Prepare for the Worst

Even with the best defenses, attacks will happen. The key is knowing how to respond quickly before things spiral out of control. Every space organization needs a Satellite Cybersecurity Incident Response Plan (SCIRP) that includes:

🔎 **Real-time threat detection** – Immediate alerts when an attack is detected.

🔎 **Isolation protocols** – Quickly shutting down compromised systems to prevent further damage.

🔎 **Recovery procedures** – Steps to regain control and restore normal satellite operations.

🔎 **Legal and compliance actions** – Understanding how to report and respond to attacks based on international cybersecurity laws.

7. International Collaboration: A United Front Against Cyber Threats

Satellites don't belong to one country—they serve global functions. So, defending them requires international cooperation. Governments, private companies, and space agencies must work together to:

☐ Create global cybersecurity standards for space systems.
☐ Share threat intelligence to detect and prevent attacks.
☐ Establish protocols for responding to space-based cyber incidents.

With space becoming the new cyber battlefield, international collaboration is no longer a nice-to-have—it's a necessity.

Final Thoughts: Space is Hard, Cybersecurity is Harder

Satellites aren't like laptops—you can't just push an update when something goes wrong. That's why proactive cybersecurity is critical. From strong encryption and AI-driven monitoring to international collaboration and secure ground stations, every layer of defense matters.

Hackers aren't waiting. Cybercriminals, nation-state actors, and rogue groups are actively exploring ways to exploit space infrastructure. The only question is: Are we prepared?

The answer better be YES, because there's no "Ctrl+Alt+Delete" in space. 🚀💀

10.2 Implementing Quantum Encryption and Advanced Cryptographic Defenses

Quantum Encryption: Because Hackers Are Already Eyeing Your Satellites

Let's face it—traditional encryption is on borrowed time. Right now, our satellite communications rely on cryptographic algorithms like RSA, ECC, and AES, which are tough to crack with today's computers. But throw a quantum computer into the mix, and suddenly, those "unbreakable" encryptions look like they were written in crayon.

Hackers love a challenge, and quantum computing is their ultimate golden ticket. With a powerful enough quantum machine, an attacker could break RSA-2048 encryption in minutes, intercepting military communications, financial transactions, and even satellite control signals.

So, what's the plan? We fight quantum with quantum. Quantum encryption isn't just another cybersecurity upgrade—it's a complete paradigm shift that will redefine how we secure space communications. Buckle up, because we're about to enter the quantum realm (no, not the Marvel one).

1. Why Traditional Encryption Will Eventually Fail

Right now, most satellite systems use public-key cryptography like RSA (Rivest-Shamir-Adleman) and ECC (Elliptic Curve Cryptography) to secure their communications. These methods rely on complex mathematical problems that are infeasible for classical computers to solve in a reasonable time.

Enter Shor's Algorithm, a quantum computing algorithm designed to crack public-key cryptography with terrifying efficiency. If a hacker with a sufficiently powerful quantum computer runs Shor's Algorithm, they can:

🚀 Decrypt satellite communication by breaking RSA encryption.

🚀 Forge cryptographic signatures, allowing unauthorized satellite commands.

🚀 Compromise secure channels used by military, government, and private space agencies.

While current quantum computers aren't powerful enough yet, companies like Google, IBM, and China's national labs are racing to build larger, more capable machines. Once they succeed, traditional encryption will crumble.

2. Quantum Encryption: The Future of Satellite Security

To counter quantum threats, researchers have developed quantum-safe encryption methods designed to resist quantum computing attacks. The two main approaches are:

A. Quantum Key Distribution (QKD): The Ultimate Eavesdropper Detector

Quantum Key Distribution (QKD) is a futuristic encryption method that uses quantum mechanics to securely distribute encryption keys. The magic happens thanks to the laws of physics, particularly the Heisenberg Uncertainty Principle and quantum entanglement.

◆ How QKD Works:

Two parties (let's call them Alice and Bob) exchange encryption keys using quantum particles (typically photons).

If an attacker (Eve) tries to intercept these keys, the quantum state of the particles changes instantly, alerting Alice and Bob to the eavesdropping attempt.

Because of this, QKD ensures that only the intended recipients receive the encryption keys, making it impossible for hackers to steal them.

🚀 **Real-world Example**: China launched the Micius satellite in 2016, which successfully demonstrated space-based QKD communications over 1,200 kilometers.

💡 **Key Advantage**: QKD is unbreakable by quantum computers because you can't copy or measure a quantum state without altering it.

B. Post-Quantum Cryptography (PQC): Quantum-Safe Encryption Without Fancy Physics

QKD is amazing, but it requires specialized quantum hardware, making it difficult to deploy globally. That's where Post-Quantum Cryptography (PQC) comes in.

PQC is a set of new cryptographic algorithms designed to withstand quantum attacks while still running on classical computers. The U.S. National Institute of Standards and

Technology (NIST) is currently finalizing the first batch of quantum-resistant encryption standards.

🚀 **Leading PQC Algorithms Include:**

🔒 **Lattice-based cryptography** – Uses hard mathematical problems that quantum computers struggle with.
🔒 **Multivariate polynomial cryptography** – Encrypts data using complex algebraic equations.
🔒 **Code-based cryptography** – Uses error-correcting codes to create unbreakable encryption.

💡 **Key Advantage**: PQC can be implemented on existing satellite systems without requiring quantum hardware, making it the most practical near-term solution.

3. Implementing Quantum Encryption for Satellites

Okay, so we know quantum encryption is the future—but how do we actually deploy it in space?

Step 1: Integrating Post-Quantum Cryptography (PQC) in Satellites

✅ Upgrade satellite firmware to support PQC algorithms (e.g., lattice-based encryption).

✅ Ensure backward compatibility with existing classical encryption.

✅ Deploy PQC-capable hardware in new satellite designs.

Step 2: Using Quantum Key Distribution (QKD) for High-Security Communications

✅ Launch QKD-enabled satellites for government, military, and financial communications.

✅ Establish a quantum-secure network between ground stations and satellites.

✅ Combine QKD with PQC for an ultra-secure hybrid encryption approach.

Step 3: Creating a Quantum-Resilient Space IoT Ecosystem

✅ Secure IoT sensors on satellites using quantum-resistant authentication.

✓ Implement AI-driven security monitoring to detect quantum-based attacks.

✓ Develop global quantum encryption standards for space agencies and private companies.

4. Challenges and Future Directions in Quantum Satellite Security

Like any cutting-edge technology, quantum encryption isn't perfect. There are still hurdles to overcome:

● **Hardware Limitations**: Quantum satellites require specialized hardware, which is expensive and difficult to manufacture.
● **Key Distribution Challenges**: QKD relies on precise optical systems that are vulnerable to environmental interference.
● **Scalability Issues**: Deploying a global quantum-secure network will take time and massive investments.

Despite these challenges, governments and companies are investing billions into quantum cybersecurity research. Organizations like NASA, DARPA, the European Space Agency (ESA), and China's quantum labs are racing to deploy quantum-resistant satellite networks.

Final Thoughts: Quantum Defense is a Space Race of Its Own

The clock is ticking. Within the next decade, quantum computers will be powerful enough to break today's encryption. The good news? We already have quantum-safe cryptographic defenses—we just need to implement them before cybercriminals and nation-state adversaries get the upper hand.

So, the next time someone says "encryption is secure," just remind them: Only until quantum says otherwise. The future of satellite security depends on how fast we move toward quantum encryption and advanced cryptographic defenses—and in this race, there's no second place. 🚀

10.3 AI-Powered Threat Detection for Space IoT Security

AI to the Rescue: Because Satellites Can't Call Tech Support

Satellites are kind of like toddlers—expensive, constantly in motion, and completely helpless when something goes wrong. Unlike a server on Earth, you can't just walk up to a satellite, plug in a USB, and run diagnostics when it starts acting weird. If a hacker sneaks into a satellite's control system or tampers with its signals, you might not even realize it until your GPS starts leading people into the ocean or a rogue weather satellite starts reporting snowstorms in the Sahara.

This is where Artificial Intelligence (AI) and Machine Learning (ML) come in. AI doesn't need coffee breaks, doesn't get bored, and can analyze vast amounts of satellite data in real-time, detecting anomalies and potential cyber threats before they cause real damage. In an era where satellites control everything from internet access to global finance and military operations, AI-powered threat detection isn't just a luxury—it's a necessity.

1. Why Traditional Security Measures Fail in Space IoT

Space IoT systems are very different from traditional IT networks. You can't just slap a firewall on a satellite and call it a day. Here's why:

🛰 **Latency Issues**: Signals between Earth and satellites take time, meaning real-time monitoring is difficult.

🛰 **Limited Processing Power**: Satellites aren't built for heavy security software; they're optimized for efficiency.

🛰 **No Physical Access**: Unlike on-ground servers, satellite hardware can't be physically inspected or rebooted easily.

🛰 **Long Lifespan with Outdated Tech**: Many satellites operate for 10+ years, meaning they often run on ancient, vulnerable systems.

🛰 **New & Evolving Threats**: Attackers are constantly innovating—from AI-driven cyberattacks to quantum hacking, the threat landscape keeps shifting.

Because of these challenges, traditional signature-based threat detection systems (which rely on pre-defined attack patterns) are useless against zero-day threats and AI-driven cyberattacks. Instead, we need AI-powered anomaly detection systems that can learn, adapt, and evolve alongside emerging threats.

2. How AI Enhances Satellite Security

AI and ML can revolutionize satellite cybersecurity by enabling real-time threat detection, automated response, and adaptive defense mechanisms. Let's break it down:

A. AI-Based Anomaly Detection

Traditional security systems look for known attack signatures (like a hacker's digital fingerprints). The problem? Hackers change tactics all the time. AI, on the other hand, detects anomalies—suspicious patterns that don't fit the satellite's normal behavior.

⬥ **Example**: If a satellite suddenly starts transmitting data to an unknown ground station in North Korea at 3 AM, AI will flag this as suspicious—even if no known signature exists for the attack.

◆ **How it Works:**

✓ AI continuously monitors satellite telemetry, communication logs, and signal integrity.

✓ It builds a "normal behavior" profile for each satellite.

✓ When something unusual happens (e.g., unexpected frequency shifts, unauthorized commands, signal spoofing), AI raises an alert.

B. Predictive Cyber Threat Intelligence

AI doesn't just detect attacks in real-time—it can also predict future attacks by analyzing trends in cyber threats.

⬥ **Example**: If AI detects that a group of satellites in a certain orbit has been targeted by DDoS attacks, it can warn other satellites in similar orbits to prepare countermeasures.

◆ **How it Works:**

✓ AI scans cybersecurity reports, dark web activity, and previous attacks.

✓ It identifies patterns in hacker behavior and predicts the next likely targets.

✓ Security teams can proactively defend satellites before attacks happen.

C. AI-Driven Intrusion Detection and Response

Satellite hacking isn't just about brute force attacks—some hackers sneak in silently, lurking in the system for weeks before striking. AI can detect these low-and-slow attacks by identifying subtle deviations in system behavior.

◆ **Example**: If a satellite control system shows a 0.5% increase in unauthorized access attempts over two months, AI will detect the gradual intrusion attempt long before a human analyst would.

◆ **How it Works:**

✓ AI constantly analyzes login patterns, command history, and system health metrics.

✓ It flags any unusual command executions (e.g., unauthorized firmware updates, rerouting of satellite signals).

✓ If an attack is detected, AI can automatically block the malicious command or isolate compromised systems.

3. Implementing AI-Based Security in Space IoT

So, how do we actually deploy AI-driven threat detection in space systems? Here's the plan:

Step 1: Embedding AI in Ground Stations

✓ Deploy AI-powered Security Operations Centers (SOCs) to monitor satellite activity in real-time.

✓ Use AI-based behavioral analytics to detect anomalies in telemetry data.

✓ Automate threat analysis using machine learning algorithms trained on historical attack data.

Step 2: Using AI at the Satellite Level

✓ Install lightweight AI models on satellite firmware to detect real-time threats (e.g., spoofed GPS signals).

✓ Implement edge AI processing to enable on-board anomaly detection without relying on ground-based analysis.

☑ Use AI to monitor power consumption, signal integrity, and system logs for cyber threats.

Step 3: AI-Driven Automated Threat Response

☑ AI should be able to automatically block unauthorized commands sent to a satellite.

☑ In case of an attack, AI can reroute communication channels to avoid compromised signals.

☑ Implement AI-driven self-healing mechanisms, allowing satellites to recover autonomously after cyber incidents.

4. Future of AI in Satellite Cybersecurity

AI is still evolving, but the future of AI-powered satellite security looks promising:

● **AI and Quantum Security**: Future AI models will work alongside quantum encryption to create ultra-secure space communications.
● **AI-Powered Swarm Defense**: AI will allow constellations of satellites to coordinate security responses as a network, rather than relying on individual defense mechanisms.
● **Deep Learning for Signal Intelligence**: AI will improve radio frequency (RF) analysis, detecting jamming, spoofing, and interference attacks faster than ever.

Final Thoughts: AI in Space – The Cybersecurity Hero We Deserve

The next generation of space cybersecurity isn't about building stronger firewalls—it's about building smarter defenses. AI gives us the ability to detect cyber threats before they strike, making it the ultimate guardian for our satellites.

So, will AI replace human cybersecurity analysts? Nope. But it will make them a thousand times more effective. And considering the ever-growing list of threats targeting space systems, I'd say we need all the AI-powered help we can get. 🚀

10.4 International Collaboration and Policy Development for Secure Space Systems

"Houston, We Have a Problem... and So Do 195 Other Countries"

If there's one thing that history has taught us, it's that humans love a good turf war—even in space. We're out here building billion-dollar satellites, launching entire constellations, and beaming internet to the remotest corners of the planet, but we still haven't figured out how to agree on basic cybersecurity rules for space systems.

Think about it: A hacker in one country could hijack a satellite owned by another, using infrastructure from a third nation, affecting services in a fourth. Who's responsible? Who enforces the law? And most importantly—how do we stop this chaotic intergalactic game of Capture the Flag before it spirals out of control?

This is why international collaboration in space cybersecurity is no longer optional. If we don't establish clear policies, the only thing protecting satellites will be hope, duct tape, and whatever encryption is still unbroken.

1. Why International Collaboration in Space Cybersecurity is Essential

Unlike Earth-based cybersecurity, where nation-states can control their own networks, space is a global commons. Every satellite, whether government-owned, commercial, or military, operates in an environment where sovereignty is blurred, and cyber threats can come from anywhere.

Here's why this matters:

☐ **No Borders in Space**: Cybercriminals, rogue states, and even "hacktivists" can target satellites from anywhere on Earth—making it impossible for a single country to secure space alone.

☐☐ **Interconnected Space IoT**: Satellite networks are deeply intertwined. A GPS outage in the U.S. could impact European banking systems, South American aviation, and Asian maritime logistics.

⚖ **Lack of Standardized Laws**: While hijacking a terrestrial network is illegal almost everywhere, hacking a satellite? The legal frameworks are vague and inconsistent across countries.

🚀 **Growing Militarization of Space**: With countries developing anti-satellite weapons (ASATs), cyberwarfare strategies, and space-based surveillance, we risk a digital arms race in orbit unless global policies are in place.

This is why governments, private companies, and international organizations need coordinated efforts to secure the future of space IoT. Otherwise, we'll be left with a digital Wild West in orbit—where the biggest hacker wins.

2. Existing International Space and Cyber Security Agreements

Despite the need for clear cybersecurity policies, international space law still hasn't caught up with modern cyber threats. Here's what we do have:

A. The Outer Space Treaty (1967)

What it says:

✓ Space is for peaceful purposes and belongs to all humankind.

✓ Countries are responsible for their national space activities, whether conducted by government agencies or private entities.

✓ No weapons of mass destruction in space.

Cybersecurity issue:

✗ The treaty never mentions cybersecurity (because, well, it was written in the 60s when "hacking" meant "chopping wood").

B. The ITU (International Telecommunication Union)

What it does:

✓ Allocates radio frequency spectrum to prevent signal interference.

✓ Ensures global coordination for satellite communications.

Cybersecurity issue:

✗ It focuses more on frequency regulation than actual cyber defense.

✗ No strict policies against spoofing, jamming, or satellite hacking.

C. The Artemis Accords (2020+)

What it does:

✓ Promotes transparency, interoperability, and peaceful space exploration.

✓ Encourages data sharing between nations.

Cybersecurity issue:

✗ Mostly about moon exploration and space resource use—doesn't directly address cyber threats.

3. The Need for New Space Cybersecurity Policies

A. Defining Cyber Crimes in Space

◆ Establish clear international definitions for cybercrimes involving satellites, including jamming, spoofing, hijacking, and data interception.

◆ Develop legal frameworks to hold nations, corporations, and individuals accountable for satellite cyberattacks.

B. Establishing Cybersecurity Standards for Satellites

◆ Countries should agree on minimum security requirements for satellites, including:

✓ End-to-end encryption for data transmission.

✓ Multi-factor authentication for satellite command access.

✓ AI-driven anomaly detection to monitor cyber threats.

◆ The ISO (International Organization for Standardization) and ITU could introduce a global cybersecurity certification for all space-based infrastructure.

C. Creating an International Space Cybersecurity Task Force

◆ Governments, space agencies (NASA, ESA, CNSA, ISRO), and private sector leaders (SpaceX, OneWeb, Amazon's Project Kuiper) must collaborate to:

✅ Share cyber threat intelligence in real time.

✅ Coordinate incident response to cyberattacks on shared satellite infrastructure.

✅ Develop joint countermeasures to defend against cyberwarfare threats.

◆ Similar to INTERPOL for cybercrime, we need an International Space Cybersecurity Agency that operates across borders.

4. Private Sector's Role in Space Cybersecurity

A. Tech Companies as Key Players

◆ Companies like SpaceX, Amazon, and Lockheed Martin are deploying thousands of satellites, making them critical stakeholders in global security.

◆ They must implement cybersecurity best practices in their satellite designs, including:

✅ Zero-trust architectures to prevent unauthorized access.

✅ AI-powered cybersecurity solutions to detect and neutralize threats autonomously.

B. Public-Private Partnerships

◆ Governments and private companies must work together to:

✅ Conduct joint cyber threat simulations.

✅ Share vulnerability disclosures to prevent large-scale attacks.

✅ Ensure secure supply chains to prevent hardware backdoors in satellite systems.

5. The Future of Global Space Cybersecurity

✒ **International Treaties 2.0**: Future agreements must specifically address cybersecurity, including rules for space-based cyberwarfare, shared security frameworks, and cooperative defense strategies.

✒ **AI-Powered Global Threat Monitoring**: Countries should invest in AI-driven space threat intelligence systems that track potential cyberattacks in real-time.

✒ **Cross-Border Cyber Defense Drills**: Just like we conduct military exercises, we need cyber defense simulations involving multiple nations to prepare for satellite-based cyber threats.

Final Thoughts: If We Don't Work Together, We All Lose

Space doesn't belong to one country, one company, or one hacker—it belongs to all of us. And if we don't figure out how to secure it collectively, we're heading toward a future where cybercriminals and rogue states could hold satellites hostage, disrupt global infrastructure, and even weaponize space IoT against us.

So, to all the world leaders, space agencies, and tech giants out there—let's stop fighting over whose satellite is bigger and start working together to make space cybersecurity a global priority. Because if we don't, the next big cyberattack might not just take down a company or a country—it might take down the entire planet. ✒💀

10.5 Future Trends and Emerging Threats in Satellite and Space IoT Cybersecurity

"The Future of Satellite Cybersecurity: More Satellites, More Problems"

You ever look up at the night sky and think, "Wow, all those twinkling lights could be streaming cat videos, guiding missiles, or getting hacked by some teenager in his basement"? No? Just me? Well, buckle up, because the future of satellite cybersecurity is looking wild.

With thousands of new satellites launching every year—thanks to companies like SpaceX, Amazon, and OneWeb—the risk of cyberattacks on space systems is skyrocketing (literally). We're talking about AI-powered satellite hacking, deepfake GPS attacks, quantum decryption nightmares, and even space-based ransomware. The threats are evolving fast, and if we don't adapt, the next major cyberwar might be fought over our heads.

So, let's take a deep dive into the future of satellite cybersecurity, the new threats we'll be facing, and how we can (hopefully) stop them before someone turns the International Space Station into a giant orbiting botnet.

1. The Future of Satellite Cybersecurity: What's Coming Next?

As satellites become smarter, more interconnected, and more essential to everything from banking to navigation, hackers are getting more creative. Here are some key trends shaping the future:

A. AI-Powered Cyberattacks on Satellites

- **AI isn't just for self-driving cars and TikTok recommendations**—it's also a powerful tool for hacking satellites.
- Future AI-powered malware could autonomously scan for vulnerabilities, exploit weaknesses, and even hide its tracks while taking over satellite systems.
- Automated hacking tools could allow nation-states and cybercriminals to launch precision satellite attacks at scale.

Possible defense? AI-powered intrusion detection systems that monitor and react in real-time to suspicious activities in satellite networks.

B. Quantum Computing vs. Satellite Encryption

- Quantum computers could break today's encryption standards in seconds, making traditional satellite security useless.
- Once quantum computing becomes mainstream, encrypted satellite data could be decrypted instantly, exposing sensitive military, financial, and communication data.
- Hackers (or rogue nations) could store intercepted satellite data now and decrypt it later when quantum computers become powerful enough (a tactic called "Harvest Now, Decrypt Later").

Possible defense? Quantum encryption and post-quantum cryptography—but we need to implement it before quantum computers go mainstream.

C. Space-Based Ransomware Attacks

If cybercriminals can lock up hospitals, banks, and energy grids with ransomware, why not satellites?

Future ransomware attacks could:

- Lock out ground stations from communicating with satellites.
- Demand millions in cryptocurrency to restore access.
- Even reroute satellites or change their orbits as a form of extortion.

Possible defense? Multi-layered access controls and strong authentication measures to prevent unauthorized command access.

D. Deepfake GPS Attacks and Fake Satellite Signals

GPS spoofing is already a major issue, but AI-generated deepfake satellite signals could take it to the next level.

Attackers could:

- Send fake GPS signals to ships, planes, and military assets, leading them off course.
- Manipulate stock markets by faking timestamps on financial transactions.
- Cause chaos in autonomous vehicles by altering navigation data.

Possible defense? Multi-constellation GNSS authentication—ensuring navigation systems compare signals from multiple independent sources to detect fakes.

E. Space Cyberwarfare and Nation-State Attacks

Countries are already testing space-based cyber weapons. Future threats include:

- Cyber weapons that can disrupt or take control of enemy satellites.
- Electromagnetic pulse (EMP) attacks that fry satellite electronics.
- Cyber-espionage satellites designed to hack or eavesdrop on communication satellites.

Possible defense? International cybersecurity treaties (if nations ever agree on them) and advanced intrusion detection systems.

2. Emerging Threats in Satellite and Space IoT Security

New threats are emerging faster than we can secure against them. Here are some of the most concerning risks on the horizon:

A. Supply Chain Attacks on Satellite Hardware

- Satellites rely on global supply chains, and attackers could insert backdoors into satellite components before launch.
- A compromised satellite chip could allow hackers to disable a satellite remotely or steal sensitive data.

Defense? Zero-trust manufacturing and hardware security audits before launch.

B. Attacks on Mega-Constellations (Starlink, OneWeb, Amazon Kuiper)

Companies like SpaceX are launching thousands of satellites to create global broadband networks.

What happens if hackers take control of a large part of the network?

- They could disrupt internet access worldwide.
- They could turn satellites into an orbiting botnet, using them to launch massive cyberattacks on Earth.

Defense? Decentralized authentication systems and rapid response teams for space-based cyber incidents.

C. Weaponized Satellites for Cyberattacks

Countries may develop satellites that can hack other satellites—think of it as offensive cyberwarfare in space.

These "cyber-killer satellites" could:

- Jam enemy satellite signals.
- Send malicious software to target satellites.
- Physically disable satellites with directed-energy weapons.

Defense? International regulations and satellite hardening techniques.

3. How We Can Prepare for Future Threats

Implement AI-Powered Cyber Defenses: If hackers use AI, we need AI-driven intrusion detection that can predict and neutralize threats before they happen.

Adopt Quantum-Resistant Cryptography: To stay ahead of quantum decryption, satellites need next-gen encryption that can't be cracked by future supercomputers.

Build Self-Healing Satellites: Future satellites could use autonomous self-repairing cybersecurity measures—like AI-driven firewalls that instantly adapt to attacks.

Global Space Cybersecurity Standards: Countries need to agree on clear cybersecurity regulations for space—before it's too late.

Final Thoughts: The Sky Isn't the Limit—It's the Battlefield

Let's be real—cybersecurity is already a mess on Earth. But in space? The stakes are even higher. If we don't act now, we're looking at a future where hackers, rogue states, and cybercriminals can manipulate global navigation, take down internet infrastructure, or even weaponize satellites against us.

So, the next time you look up at the night sky, just remember: those aren't just stars—they're potential cyberwarfare battlegrounds. And if we don't get serious about securing them, we might wake up one day to a world where the hackers control the heavens.

Well, here we are—at the end of a wild ride through the chaotic, fascinating, and sometimes downright ridiculous world of satellite hacking. If you've made it this far, congratulations! You now know more about breaking, securing, and understanding space IoT systems than 99% of the population (including some people who actually work in the industry). I mean, who needs Hollywood when real-life hackers are out here spoofing GPS signals, hijacking satellite uplinks, and jamming entire communication networks?

From sniffing out satellite signals in your backyard to reverse-engineering firmware that was probably written decades ago by someone who definitely didn't have cybersecurity in mind, we've covered everything you need to know about offensive and defensive satellite security. We've exposed weak encryption, insecure ground stations, shady nation-state cyberwarfare tactics, and, of course, how to protect satellites from all of the above.

But here's the thing—this isn't the end. If there's one lesson you should take away from this book, it's that security is a constantly moving target. The moment we think we've locked everything down, some clever hacker (maybe even you!) finds a new way in. That's why learning never stops—which is exactly why I created the IoT Red Teaming: Offensive and Defensive Strategies series. If you enjoyed this deep dive into satellite hacking, then trust me, you're going to love the rest of the series.

Maybe *Mastering Hardware Hacking* is more your thing—where we crack open embedded systems like Christmas presents. Or perhaps *Wireless Hacking Unleashed* is calling your name, where we dive into *Wi-Fi, Bluetooth, and RF exploits* that make even the most secure networks tremble. Feeling a bit more down to earth? The Car Hacker's Guide is a must-read if you want to understand how to break (or protect) modern vehicles. And if you're really into chaos, *Drone Hacking and Hacking Medical IoT* are packed with exploits that will make you look at UAVs and smart hospitals in a whole new (terrifying) way.

To everyone who picked up this book, thank you. Whether you're a security researcher, pentester, space enthusiast, or just a curious hacker who got sucked into the world of satellite cybersecurity, I appreciate you taking the time to go on this journey with me. Your curiosity, passion, and willingness to learn are what push the field forward. The more we understand about how things break, the better we can secure the technology that shapes our world (and beyond).

So what's next? More hacking, more learning, and hopefully fewer satellites getting hijacked. Keep exploring, stay curious, and maybe—just maybe—one day you'll be the one securing the future of space technology. Or at the very least, you'll know how to stop the bad guys from turning a weather satellite into their personal DJ station.

Until next time—hack the world, secure the future, and don't get caught.

– *Zephyrion Stravos*

www.ingramcontent.com/pod-product-compliance
Lightning Source LLC
LaVergne TN
LVHW081754050326
832903LV00027B/1943